THE OTHER SIDE OF
THIS

By

Dr. Jacqueline E. McCullough

Includes Workbook Supplement

The Other Side of This

Table of Contents

The Other Side of This

Acknowledgements

I am so grateful to the Lord for His kindness and grace towards me. I give Him all the glory, the honor and praise. I dedicate this book to my mother, Evangelist Keturah Elizabeth Phillips, who is now 100 years and several months. She has been my greatest supporter, intercessor and friend. I offer this book in the precious memory of my father, the Rev. Percival Gravel Heron Phillips, who always encouraged me to give all to my Lord and Savior.

I would like to thank Pastor Robyn Edwards, Rev. Trish McLeod and Rev. Amie Gardner, who assisted me in bringing this work into fruition. I thank my church family Beth Rapha for their prayers and support as Pastor and Founder. Thanks to all the Rapha Alliance members and their churches, especially Pastors Benton, at Greater Bethel in Cincinnati, OH.

I devote this work to my goddaughter, Alexandria Cross and her children, Jaylah and Josh Jr. I also dedicate this book to baby Grace Olivia Pope, parented by Rufus and Sonja Pope; to Jordan Christopher and Gianna Christine Guercy, parented by Robertson and Tracee-Anne Guercy; and to Caleb Bryce and Evan Taylor Bullock, parented by Colette and Carlos Bullock. To all those who will be blessed by this book, I send you God's blessings!

The Other Side of This

Introduction

God has a way of illustrating our existence with colorful hues; shades of gray, white, blue, black, green, yellow, and red reflect the high and low points of our existence. These colors evoke memories of favorable and unfavorable experiences. As I reflect, I acknowledge that my life has certainly floated through the realm of change both rapidly and timelessly.

There were days when I did not know whether the clock continued to tick, or if I missed a whole day in the passage of time. My journey and your journey is what life is all about. Life here on Earth continues to evolve into pages and volumes of feelings, expressions, emotions, insights, regrets and joys. These diverse experiences all add up to who and where we are, moment by moment. Where we are is our spiritual location and how we perceive God. How we respond to the experiences we have on our respective journeys determines our perception of God. Our responses to our circumstances determine whether we see Him as good, evil, indifferent, or loving.

The Other Side of This

A Matter of Perception

I went on my first vacation in many years with some friends. We had arranged to go on a Caribbean cruise. It had been a long time since my last vacation, and I was filled with anticipation and joy. My friends and I flew out on the first leg of our journey expecting to catch a connecting flight to Puerto Rico, but the connecting flight was delayed more than four hours; consequently we missed our cruise connection. Exhausted and deeply disappointed, my first thought was that this was the devil. There must have been a flaw in the planning; after all, we had all booked our own travel. Maybe someone more experienced would have anticipated the delay.

I was let-down and frustrated. Because none of us were travel agents, making further accommodations was even more burdensome. Then, without much warning, we had to hurriedly board a flight to St. Thomas in hopes of making a rendezvous with our cruise ship. Finally, I took a moment and quieted my spirit — which was an intentional act, not a reaction — and I realized that God had a purpose in allowing the delay. I had to stop reacting, because until then, my expectations were disappointed and I was reacting out of emotion.

Our reactions are emotional and they are usually different from a godly response. A godly response would have required me to allow God's purpose to come forward. I wanted God's purpose, so gradually I calmed myself and waited expectantly for God. How wonderful He is! When we arrived in St. Thomas, we were assigned a trip coordinator, who arranged all our travel.

The cruise line was very apologetic and refunded us the cost of our missed day.

The rest of our vacation was wonderful and free from unpleasant surprises. Our very able cruise coordinator helped us enjoy every aspect of the cruise, even things we might have missed. The delay provided us with an opportunity to fully enjoy our trip, but the key was hidden in a challenging spiritual place. It is difficult to control an emotional reaction, because emotions are powerful. Yet, a godly response will put God in control — and that changed my entire spiritual location. My new spiritual location allowed me to see a loving God, Who was eager to help me have a restful, pleasant vacation. Our spiritual location determines how we see God.

I am not a philosopher, but as a preacher I have journeyed with intention through the moments of my life. By intention, I mean that I have consciously chosen to follow a godly response rather than an emotional reaction when there was or is trouble on my journey. I have also been graced with the opportunity to take excursions with many others as they hasten through their process of living. The issue for many of us is that our lives do not always fit into a pattern that easily unfolds its meaning, beauty, purpose, or ultimately, satisfaction. It is our quest to find answers to why the colors in our lives are hazy, shapes are convoluted, movements are abrupt and clumsy, touches are unhealthy, experiences are painful, and our connections to one another are so disappointing that they cause many of us to frown on some of the most important experiences in our lives.

The Other Side of This

In my walk with the Lord and my vocation as a minister, I am confronted, not only with my own "whys?" but also with the "whys?" of others. It can be terribly frustrating to try to analyze and seek the meaning for every experience in life. It is even more mind-boggling to attempt to give reasons and explanations for these occurrences. Yet, it is a fact that we are limited as humans. We lack so much information and we are so confined to our own world that we cannot justify our own motivations and behaviors. If we can't even fully understand our own behavior, how can we possibly understand God?

The anguish we experience is sometimes so great that it is impossible not to be overwhelmed by emotion. I am reminded of one of my own inexplicable moments of grief, when after a full-term, healthy pregnancy, my baby girl, Myette Charisse McCullough, died three hours after birth. Yet, I cannot say that God did not speak to me during the pregnancy and warn me, in more ways than one, that my baby would fly out of my life suddenly. It was not the information that was overwhelming; it was my human inability to comprehend the incomprehensible plan and ways of God in my life that made the experience so overwhelming.

As a pastor and a biblical counselor, I know that every life has moments and times when words escape us and thoughts flee from us because the emotion of the circumstance is so overwhelming. Pain of such great intensity can even cause us to have negative thoughts about God, hurl accusations against Him, or even cause us to entertain thoughts of denouncing Him. You are not alone!

Dr. Jacqueline E. McCullough

There is another side to "this"! No matter what "this" is, your life is worth more than "this" experience you are facing right now! Job thought that his life was inexplicably torn apart in 24 hours for no reason, but at the end of the book of Job in Chapter 42:1-6, he made this remarkable declaration:

> Then Job replied to the LORD: "I know that you can do all things; no plan of yours can be thwarted. [You asked,] 'Who is this that obscures my counsel without knowledge?' Surely I spoke of things I did not understand, things too wonderful for me to know. [You said,] 'Listen now, and I will speak; I will question you, and you shall answer me.' My ears had heard of you but now my eyes have seen you. Therefore I despise myself and repent in dust and ashes."

I want you to glide through this book, using it as an index to the volume of pages in your journal of life. Let these writings, along with prayer and the Word of God, guide you to the other side of your "this." "This" may be the time you have been waiting for to shift you into appreciating your God, your life and your purpose on Earth. Read and expect to see more deeply into the purposes of God in your life, and gain another perspective on your suffering and the other side of "this"!

The Other Side of This

The Holding Pattern

I am what you would call a "frequent flyer." Quite often I even fly across the globe. To some people that sounds exciting, but as most seasoned travelers know, it can abruptly become quite challenging. While traveling to Baltimore on January 27, 1986, to speak at the renowned Bethel A.M.E. Church, where the Rev. Drs. John and Cecilia Bryant were the pastors, I was confronted with something that every airline passenger dreads. It was a chilly, wintry night, and I caught the last flight heading to Baltimore. That flight is clearly etched in my memory because in all the years that I have travelled across the globe, I have never had a more frightening one.

As a frequent flyer, I am not afraid of flying, but I have never been comfortable with turbulence — the drops and dips that planes make while airborne. But this was beyond ordinary turbulence; this entire flight had an aura of gloom and doom. I sensed that something was wrong and that the atmosphere was troubled. As the bouncing, dipping and shaking intensified, I grabbed the hand of the gentleman who was sitting next to me, and started praying. It seems hard to imagine anything more unsettling than violent turbulence, but the thing that disturbed me most was the holding pattern of the flight, which continued in a wide uneven arc around the airport for nearly an hour.

Jostling about in stagnant air, and sitting in an airplane with the engines droning on a circular path to nowhere, I knew that the threat of death was lurking. My sense of foreboding continued even after we landed and sat in the motionless stuffy plane waiting to deplane.

The next morning, my suspicions were confirmed when I heard that the spaceship Challenger had exploded upon takeoff on Tuesday, January 28, 1986.

In our lives, there are times when our holding patterns indicate danger and destruction afoot. On that flight, my sense of unease was due to the combined factors of unusually heavy turbulence, and a frighteningly long delay. Even though I was not aware of every aspect of the situation, I had a sense something outside of my control that had gone terribly wrong. Unknown to me, our country was experiencing a national tragedy. A terrible fate had befallen the astronauts on the space shuttle Challenger and initially no one knew why. Air traffic controllers around our nation's capital must have been in a quandary as the aviation industry sought to ensure that all was safe. But as a passenger on my flight, all I had was a terrible sense of discomfort and foreboding.

Under those circumstances, "this" experience for me was very hard to understand. Confronted with this frightening situation, I had to try to figure things out as best I could. For me, prayer was a natural and immediate way to relieve the mounting tension and fear. In "this" situation, and without any other information, my emotional make-up, the information I could glean from my surroundings, my predispositions, and my spiritual maturity all played a role in determining my internal state and my external responses. As Christians, our priorities are constantly challenged.

Can we really trust God to bring us through situations that we perceive (or that anyone would perceive) as terrifying, humiliating or painful? God's Word says:

> "Dear friends, do not be surprised at the painful trial you are suffering as though something strange were happening to you. But rejoice that you participate in the sufferings of Christ, so that you may be overjoyed when His glory is revealed" (2 Peter 4:12-13).

Safe People

Our emotional make-up is something that we receive at birth. Our inclinations towards certain behaviors can be influenced by our surroundings. A childhood trauma can make us more vulnerable, but one of the most critical factors that influence our predispositions and emotional tendencies are the people to whom we talk. These people that we confide in and trust become our "interpreters." Often, they inform our thoughts and emotions as much and sometimes more than the things we see with our own eyes. There are times, however, that our interpreters are not helpful because they bring their own perspectives and predispositions to our situations.

For example, a person whose marriage has been destroyed by infidelity and deceit may be a very poor interpreter of your marital circumstances. Even if you are not terribly jealous of your spouse and see no real reason to be, how can a person who is looking for deception and betrayal everywhere and in everything possibly help you see more clearly? Such a person, if they refuse to embrace their healing, can only make you more insecure. Scripture warns us: "Blessed is the man who does not walk in the counsel of the wicked or stand in the way of sinners or sit in the seat of mockers" (Psalm 1:1).

But it is often the case that our interpreters are people who we trust and look to for emotional and moral support. How can we know whether our interpreters are trustworthy and safe? Here is a simple definition: *Safe people lead us toward Christ.*

These people may not be perfect and may have flaws, but if they are consistently leading you to Jesus, they are safe. Unsafe people are often critical, irresponsible, and unwilling to stick around when the situation gets more difficult. The Bible describes safe people in 2nd Corinthians as those who "praise God, the Father of our Lord Jesus, who is: the Father of compassion and the God of all comfort, who comforts us in all our trouble, so that we can comfort those in any trouble with the comfort we ourselves have received from God" (2 Corinthians 1:3-4). Safe people have already overcome some of their insecurities and past traumas and have been comforted by Jesus. Because they know God's comfort and reassurance, they can pass it along. Safe people can give perspective, without demoralizing.

But what if "this" experience seems so much greater and lasting than just a frightening moment or a missed opportunity? The same principles still apply. It is tempting to get into a comparison of suffering, but it does not help. For some of us, losing a job is as devastating as a divorce. For others, losing another friendship is as devastating as losing a spouse. How we perceive what happens to us depends on the same factors: our emotional make-up, our predispositions, our experiences, our environments and our spiritual maturity. One person might be on the verge of suicide over losing a job, where another person may feel that the same job is of little value and could quit without any concern. Likewise, a person who is not ready to be a parent may be secretly relieved at the loss of a child where another person may be horribly, inconsolably distressed. Emotional make-up, background, and environment all have a role in our internal perceptions. We may not have as much control as we would like over those factors, but we have a lot of control over our ability to achieve a degree of spiritual maturity.

A spiritually mature person must have a measure of self-discipline and a willingness to have a submitted relationship with Jesus. Spiritual maturity and what we usually call spirituality in the Church differ significantly. What often passes for spirituality is emotionalism or mechanical memorization of a lot of Scripture. The bottom line truth is: *You are as spiritual as you are obedient to God.* You are as spiritually mature as you are willing to submit to God.

For example, you can nurse an insult or grudge for years, but in order to mature spiritually, you must confront the problem, and either release the person, or forgive them, or both. When the Bible requires us as Christians to show forgiveness, it is a clear command: "Whenever you stand praying, forgive, if you have anything against anyone; so that your Father, who is in heaven, may also forgive you your transgressions" (Mark 11:25). Genuine forgiveness is a sign of true spiritual maturity. We don't forgive because it is not in our nature to do so. However, we forgive because we have subjected our nature to God's will. That's why Jesus said, "If you love me, keep my commands" (John 14:15). But how do we accomplish such a challenging feat as setting our feelings aside? The Apostle Paul tells us: "We demolish arguments and every pretension that sets itself up against the knowledge of God, and we take captive every thought to make it obedient to Christ" (2 Corinthians 10:5). Again, you are spiritually mature when you are willing to submit to God.

There are also times when we are not ready to "land" because there are other things that are not in place. Because we don't know all, see all, or understand everything, we are reduced to interpreting what we do know, see and understand. Our perspective is limited and our knowledge is incomplete. We are not aware of the hidden opportunities that await us and the circumstances God has prepared for us. Our inclination is to call something that we don't fully understand a negative event before we can see the full picture. The holding pattern that we call a "delayed opportunity" can actually be God's intended blessing. We can receive His comfort knowing that He says, "I know the thoughts I have for you..." (Jeremiah 29:29).

There are quite a few airports that are extremely congested during certain times of the day and seasons of the year. New York and New Jersey airports are extremely susceptible to air traffic congestion. Major cities like Chicago, Washington, DC, Los Angeles, and Dallas also have airports that are prone to overcrowding, causing flights to be delayed in holding patterns. As it is in the natural, so it is in the spiritual. There are times and places when holding patterns are part of our reality.

Are you experiencing a holding pattern in your life? Is everything in your life silent, causing you to feel hindered, aimless and arrested in your daily life? Well, let's see if these holding patterns can prepare us for the other side of "this."

The Place of Transition

The Federal Aviation Administration Handbook defines a *holding pattern* as "a predetermined maneuver designed to keep an aircraft within a specified airspace." These procedures are designated to absorb flight delays that may occur on an airway, during terminal arrival and on missed approach.[1]

The FAA definition seems to have three parts. The first part is that it is a *procedure.* The procedure is very specific: safety in the air, time efficiency, and successful landing on arrival. It's a process!

---

[1] "The Federal Aviation Adminstration Handbook (New York, NY: Skyhorse Publishing, 2008), http://www.faa.gov/regulations_policies/orders_notices/index.cfm/go/document.information/documentID/10408

When a plane is in a holding pattern in the air, it is essentially in a "transitional place" between reaching its destination and landing on the airfield. Transitions are extremely difficult.

The Bible contains one of the most historically, spiritually and personally significant accounts of transition in human history—the Exodus from Egypt. The ancient Hebrews had to wander for *40 years*! That is a long transition, but God knew that until the people were ready to enter the Land of Promise, He couldn't allow them to enter; the time had to be right. In fact, the entire generation of ancient Israelites that left Egypt had to die (except for Caleb and Joshua) before a new generation could enter the land. The previous generation did not exhibit the ability to be spiritually mature (i.e., obedient to God), so a new generation which was more mature spiritually had to replace them.

Despite their rebellion and disobedience in that transition time, God did not abandon the people, but provided for and protected them. He fed them with manna from heaven and quail. Their sandals never wore out despite all of their travels. A "holding pattern" describes perfectly what God does for us in a time of transition, because He has "predetermined maneuvers designed" to keep us exactly where we should be.

Another well-known example of God protecting His people in a place of safety during a transition is Noah in the ark. God had chosen to save a remnant of fallen humanity, and Noah was the last spiritually mature person on earth. Noah demonstrated his spiritual maturity by building a huge ark on dry land. For 100 years, Noah was the object of ridicule and scorn as he obeyed God's command to build. Finally, the rains came.

Noah and his family were safe in the ark while the rest of humankind perished. Although the ark was safe, it was filled with animals. It had few amenities, and no rudder! Noah was in a difficult "holding pattern." He was safe and secure, but not comfortable.

Scripture says, "[he] who dwells in the shelter of the Most High will rest in the shadow of the Almighty" (Psalm 91:1). God has a specific "airspace" in which to keep us, which is part of His process for bringing us safely to a landing space.

The second aspect of the holding pattern is the *plan*. It is not a whim or a fluke. It is a safety measure that is built into the system of flight to protect passengers from danger and to prevent unnecessary delays. This plan would include all the preparation of the ground crew, the airline staff, the flight crew, pilot and the air traffic controllers — all the things passengers don't think about. God has a plan and He is preparing things for us when we land. While we are in transition, we can either choose to be anxious, or we can take the opportunity to prepare for landing by spiritually maturing (i.e., drawing closer to God and learning to trust Him).

The third aspect of the definition is that successfully being in a holding pattern requires *patience*. The element of waiting or being purposefully delayed is the central theme in the experience of the holding pattern. As we come to understand the holding pattern from a variety of perspectives, we begin to recognize that the holding pattern has been preordained to protect us! Can you be patient if it requires that you just trust and wait, even when you do not understand or agree with the decision? Remember, the test of spiritual maturity is willingness to submit to God! This is the key to getting the most out of your holding pattern.

There is an alternate definition of a holding pattern that states that a holding pattern is: "[a] state or period of no progress or change."[2] I used to hate the word "wait" in the early days of my Christian journey. Like many of us, I resented not being in control. We often feel anxious or resentful when we're in a holding pattern. What a waste of time it is to assume that because we are not in control that there is "no progress or change" happening. From that perspective, we lose a valuable opportunity to draw closer to God and reap all the benefits of a relationship with Him. Now, in retrospect, I am more appreciative of the process of waiting; yet, even now, I still have to speak to my spirit and keep it from racing beyond the boundaries of God's divine timing.

Timing is everything. Time is our most valuable commodity. Yet many of us are racing against time or mismanaging it. The quest to control our time is indicative of our need to be in control of our lives. Our desire to be in control is in the nature of our being. We want to know, we want to be in charge, we want to drive the car, and we want to fly the plane. It is when the plane halts, circles in a pattern, and does not move into position to land that we become unnerved. I am

---

[2] Simpson, John; Weiner, Edmund, Ed. "Oxford Dictionaries." Oxford University Press, 1989. Web. 1 Feb 2012. *http://oxforddictionaries.com/definition/holding pattern?region=us.*

convinced that waiting patiently is one of the virtues that many Christians are least likely to embrace.

Learning to wait patiently takes self-discipline. Scripture acknowledges how difficult it is to become disciplined. In The Epistle to the Hebrews, it says: "No discipline seems pleasant at the time, but painful. Later on, however, it produces a harvest of righteousness and peace for those who have been trained by it" (Hebrews 12:11).

Having the self-discipline to be patient in adversity has an additional benefit; it builds character. If we can be self-disciplined enough to wait patiently, God reveals His wonderful plan at exactly the right moment. With deeper insight and a better-developed character, we can appreciate more fully the awesome and wonderful things God has for each one of us.

I have had my bouts of intolerance and impatience with God's plan, purpose, and timing in my life. I especially remember my quest to obtain a graduate degree, which I hoped would refine my educational experience. For as long as I could remember, I had always wanted to be a medical doctor. When I was still a child on the Island of Jamaica, I used to tell my parents that when I became of age, I was going to open up a doctor's office and take care of all the sick people in the neighborhood. We migrated from Jamaica, West Indies, to the United States, and that dream lingered in my breast. I went through elementary, middle, and high school with that zeal burning in my heart. I embarked on my journey by going to nursing school. Upon graduation, I intentionally planned to smoothly transition from nursing into medical school.

It almost happened. I worked at Harlem Hospital, and, during my sixth year, I planned to leave my position and return to school. I was ready to take the classes necessary to finish my pre-med requirements and then go on to medical school. One day, shortly after I made my decision, I went to prayer and the Lord spoke clearly to me and said, "Take off your lab coat, for I am calling you into full-time ministry!" These words shook every fiber of my being. In fact, I was so shaken by the Lord's command that it caused me to doubt my sanity.

Could it be possible that my childhood dream would have to be abandoned at this point in my life? I wept profusely and became extremely depressed. It took a dear friend and mentor, Evangelist Shirley Watson, to walk me through my surrender to God's will.

Even though I obeyed, I still moped and grumbled occasionally about the interruption of my educational pursuit. It took years to settle my mind and calm my spirit (about something that was already quite clear) concerning God's expressed will for my life. The Lord, Who is ever mindful of our pain, revisited me on this issue. He knew my desire to be a doctor and assured me that one day I would be a doctor, but a doctor in ministry and not a medical doctor. It was about 15 years or so later that those words from God came to me. The power and reassurance of those words guided me and I graduated from Drew Theological Seminary with a Doctorate in Ministry on May 21, 2005.

The holding pattern was long, but the landing was on time.

The landing also had more profound meaning attached to it. My landing actually combined ministry and medicine. Since 1997, our evangelistic ministry and more recently, The International Gathering at Beth Rapha (the church where I pastor) have been involved in bringing medical clinics to the Island of Jamaica. This mammoth undertaking has ministered to over 30,000 people and has blessed the Island with over $1 million worth of food, medicine, medical equipment and services. It was not until my fourth visit to the Island that it dawned on me that my plane had landed and my holding pattern was truly over. God gave me the opportunity to bring a fine medical staff and wonderful volunteers to give hope, love, and medicine to His people. This ministry was more far-reaching than any private medical practice could ever have been. I saw the purpose for the hold-up and the hold-back. It was to prepare me to accomplish greater and reach farther for the Kingdom of God.

But how was I able to hear God's voice at that critical time in my life? How could I distinguish the voice of God from the voice of my own ambition? In order to know God and what He requires, we have to know His precious Word. There are so many Bible characters whose lives were transitioned by God from one season into the next for His glory.

Divine Selection in Transition

For example, Esther, whose name means, "star,"[3] and whose Hebrew name was Hadassah, experienced the Lord's divine selection for His purpose. She was an orphan who was cared for by her cousin Mordecai in the midst of the people of Israel who were exiled and oppressed. She was from an oppressed people at a terrible time in their history, and she was without a name or a distinction.

Yet providentially, this young girl was pulled from one of the 127 provinces ruled by the Medo-Persian Empire and was groomed as the next queen for the King of Persia, Artaxerxes. For one year, she was tutored, coached and prepared, physically, emotionally and culturally, after which she was presented to the king. She was chosen, not merely for fame or fancy, but because God placed her so that she would aid in the redemption, protection, and preservation of the Jewish people under a foreign leadership. God told her that she had come to her position as queen precisely "for such a time as this." God is timely and purposeful!

The lives of the Jews were threatened by a sinister edict put forth and instigated by one of the king's chief men, Haman the Agagite. Haman was the embodiment of an ancient enemy of the Israelites. Amalekite by birth, Haman the Agagite was born from the descendants of Agag, an insidious and historic Canaanite enemy of Israel. When Israel first emerged from Egypt and journeyed through the wilderness, the

---

[3] Pfeiffer, Charles F. *Wycliffe Bible Dictionary* (Peabody, MA: Hendrickson Publishers, 1989), p. 548.

Agagites opposed them and sought the destruction of Israel (see Exodus 17). As a result, the Lord decreed judgment against the Amalekites, and that judgment came to its fulfillment in Amalek's conflict with Israel during the time of the prophet Samuel and King Saul (see 1 Samuel 15). The clan of Agag was especially hateful in their opposition to Israel. It was an ancient and bitter animosity that lingered between the Agagites and the people of God.

Consequently, Haman deeply resented the Jews, especially Mordecai, because they did not bow and genuflect before him. The Jews were in exile because they had disobeyed God and submitted themselves to idol worship. The bitterness of exile caused the Jews to realize the error of their ways. So Mordecai, like many of his fellow Jews, refused to submit himself to the worship of any idol. This act of devotion to their covenant God in a heathen kingdom infuriated Haman. Through political maneuvering, he asked the king to wipe out the Jews by making a proclamation for their destruction.

In the face of the edict against the Jews, issued with the authority of the king, Mordecai invoked Queen Esther's aid, asking her to intercede before the king for her people. The problem was that no one came before the king without being invited. To demand an audience with the king was considered an insult, and could be punishable by death. Only if the king extended his scepter inviting the visit would the person's life be spared. Esther would be taking her life in her hands if she approached the king to plead for her people. Because she had not recently been in the king's presence, she became afraid, knowing that it was not customary for her to see the king without his invitation. Yet she was challenged to accept an unavoidable assignment, which was so pointedly stated by Mordecai in the Book of Esther, Chapter 4:13-14:

> "Do not think that because you are in the king's house you alone of all the Jews will escape. For if you remain silent at this time, relief and deliverance for the Jews will arise from another place, but you and your father's family will perish. And who knows but that you have come to royal position for such a time as this?"

Esther suddenly realized that her "plane" was now "landing." Her "holding pattern" and her time of existing without a true sense of purpose were over. She connected her assignment with her purpose for being in the palace. In Esther 4:16, she gave an astoundingly selfless response, saying:

> "Go, gather together all the Jews who are in Susa, and fast for me. Do not eat or drink for three days, night or day. I and my maids will fast as you do. When this is done, I will go to the king, even though it is against the law. And if I perish, I perish."

The word "perish" in the original Hebrew means that if she were annihilated, she would be willing to suffer the punishment for her people.[4]

"This" holding pattern can come with much confusion and disillusionment because it seems to be going nowhere. But in our lives, just as in the life of

---

[4] Baker, Warren; Carpenter, Eugene. *The Complete Word Study Dictionary Old Testament* (Chattanooga, TN: AMG Publishers, 2003). Hebrew word: *abad, STC# 6*, p. 1.

Esther, we can feel trapped in "this"; yet every moment, change, and insignificant move is leading to something or somewhere far greater than we can ever imagine — if we can just wait patiently. The reality is, we have to wait if we are in a plane's holding pattern in order to be able to land safely. The only alternative would be to jump out of the plane.

There is really nothing else to do but wait. The issue is *how* we should wait.

What to Do in the Wait

According to Barnes' commentary, the psalmist utters a word of encouragement in Psalm 33:20 to those who are waiting: "Our soul waiteth for the LORD: he is our help and our shield."[5] *Strong's Exhaustive Concordance* states that this word "wait" in Hebrew is *chakah*, which means "to tarry, to long for."[6] We are not waiting for human intervention, but we are waiting on the LORD. He is our Help [or] our Rescuer; He is our Protection, and He is our Preserver.

The other side of your "this" will unfold, but only after you have patiently waited for the opportunity to land from a holding pattern. What is the difference between waiting and waiting patiently? Just waiting without self-discipline is stagnation. Stagnant, passive waiting can be "depression in a low tone," that is,

[5] Barnes, Albert. *Barnes' Notes On The Old Testament, Psalms Vol. I* (Grand Rapids, MI: Baker Book House, 1998), p. 284.

[6] Baker, Warren; Carpenter, Eugene. *The Complete Word Study Dictionary Old Testament* (Chattanooga, TN: AMG Publishers, 2003). Hebrew word: *hakah, STC# 2442*, p. 336.

depression undercover. In other words, the attitude becomes, "If I can't have what I want, then I don't want anything." There is an aspect of anger in this kind of waiting. There is an assumption that "if I could just take control," this wait would be over; but since I can't, I'll just "stew."

Passive-aggressive behavior can be a result of this mindset and is a veiled attempt to hide feelings of helplessness, anger and aggression. While suppressing overt expressions of negative feelings, one resorts to covert means. "Stewing" in anger, waiting for opportunities to express rage, refusing to assume responsibilities, and being envious and hypercritical of others are all ways that we can express our dissatisfaction with waiting in a holding pattern.

Stagnant, angry, passive waiting won't make your landing happen any sooner. In fact, it may delay it even more.

How should we be waiting then? Taking control of our emotional reactions is the first step. Then we must become disciplined, recognizing that *waiting doesn't mean that we should stop living!* Throughout both letters to the Thessalonians, Paul encourages the early Church to actively wait for Jesus to return,

> "Make it your ambition to lead a quiet life, to mind your business and to work with your hands, just as we told you" (1 Thessalonians 4:11).

> "And we urge you, brothers, warn those who are idle, encourage the timid, help the weak, be patient with everyone" (1 Thessalonians 5:14).

Paul continues to strongly encourage the Thessalonians to avoid idleness as they wait, saying, "In the name of the Lord Jesus Christ, we command you brothers, to keep away from every brother who is idle and does not live according to the teaching you received from us." (2 Thessalonians 3:6). He even goes so far as to say, "If a man will not work, he shall not eat" (2 Thessalonians 3:10). Active waiting requires us to discipline our emotions and impulses; it requires us to do our work, having faith in God's ability to bring us to exactly the "landing" that will fulfill and satisfy us.

Look around you now and assess your holding pattern. Identify what your "this" is. It could be that you are waiting for a job for a long period of time. You may be going through a long convalescence, or you could be trusting God for the salvation of a loved one. These are just a few of the many "holding patterns" presented in our lives that confront us daily and seem to stifle our hopes and dreams.

Yet God says to wait and trust His Word. He has a master plan and it is much more than the eye can see. Commit your heart anew to His purpose and plan, and allow Him to temper your heart, mind, spirit and desires to conform to His divine timing. God is sovereign. If we want to survive our "holding pattern," and land exactly where we should at the perfect time, we have to trust a power beyond ourselves — we have to trust God. When we are truly in a "holding pattern," we can do absolutely nothing. None of our resources can alter our situation. For Christians, this is the moment when we have to let go of our need to be in control and fully believe that God is in control. If our faith in God is real, this realization should move us into a place of comfort and protection.

What if things aren't so bad? What if the holding pattern has gotten comfortable? Even when we feel all is well, life can be filled with swift and sudden changes. Things that no one could have imagined can occur in the blink of an eye. On Tuesday, September 11, 2001, at 7 a.m., Eastern Standard Time, no one could have imagined what lay in store for us — the tragedy of the destruction of the Twin Towers in New York City, and the loss of so many lives.

God is able, not only to get us through the terrifying and unexpected things that happen in our lives, He also protects us from innumerable dangers we don't even know about. For example, NASA maintains a website on "Near-Earth Objects,"[7] which are meteors that are approaching and coming close enough to the earth to detect. These objects range in size from a few meters to three or four kilometers.

Although a large meteor striking the earth could devastate human existence, we have little or no awareness of this constant danger. But God protects us, whether we know it or not. When we fail to consider God's continuous protection, we not only deceive ourselves, but we are denying the vast and wonderful benefits that come to us from God. Scripture says, "The fool says in his heart 'there is no God'" (Psalm 53:1). No one who knows better should want to be a fool.

God controls so much more than we can ever imagine. It is our ability to understand the vast goodness of God that is limited. Admittedly, we can develop our character if we choose to wait patiently, but

---

[7] Near-Earth Object Program: neo.jpl.nasa.gov

good character is a mere by-product. The most significant benefit we can derive from patient and submitted waiting is the ability to acknowledge God.

When Nicodemus, a member of the Jewish ruling counsel, came to Jesus, he acknowledged Jesus' profound ability, saying, "We know you are a teacher and you come from God. For no one can perform the miraculous signs you are doing if God were not with him." Yet Jesus replied, "I tell you the truth, no one can see the kingdom of God unless he is born again" (John 3:3). Jesus told Nicodemus what must be done when we acknowledge God. By acknowledging God, we become able to see the Kingdom of God — all the vast number of things and situations that are under God's control. Can we go to Heaven without God? Can we live eternally without God?

When we can see the truth of these things, we naturally desire to access our Wonderful God. How, then, would we be able to get to God? How are we able to commune and be in fellowship with Him? Jesus said, "I am the way the truth and the life. No one comes to the Father except through me" (John 14:6). When we accept Jesus Christ, we have God.

His omniscience, His power, and His comfort are all ours if we acknowledge, accept, and love Him. It is then that we will be able to experience true fulfillment as we walk in full obedience and submission to Him. The greatest benefit that comes to me when I am stuck in the "holding patterns" of life is that if I have God living in my life — I will get to the other side of "this."

The Holding Patterns

What Is This? (Identifying your "this" situations)

1. After reading Chapter One, see if you can identify the different "holding pattern" situations in your life. Make a list of those that you have been waiting on the Lord to change.

_____

_____

_____

_____

_____

2. Describe those "holding pattern" situations in detail, and the frightening and unpredictable circumstances that have you feeling as if you're suspended in midair.

_____

_____

_____

_____

_____

_____

_____

3. What is your biggest fear in these situations?

_____

_____

_____

_____

_____

_____

4. We all go through different things from time to time, but it's important to use the support that God has given. Who are some of the people that you have connected with as "interpreters"? How do you know that they are God-given support? How have they helped you, if at all?

_____

_____

_____

_____

_____

_____

_____

_____

_____

Spiritual Maturity

1. Are you still holding people hostage for things done to you? Make a list of those persons.

_____

_____

_____

_____

_____

_____

_____

_____

2. Based on Mark 11:25, John 14:15 and 2 Corinthians 10:5, what is your plan of action regarding these people?

_____

_____

_____

_____

_____

_____

_____

_____

_____

3. How is this situation teaching you to trust God and draw closer to Him?

_____

_____

_____

_____

_____

4. How have you grown in your level of patience?

_____

_____

_____

_____

_____

_____

Personal Inventory

"How should we be waiting? Taking control of our emotional reactions is the first step, and then being disciplined and recognizing that waiting doesn't mean stop living!" Paul encourages the early Church to actively wait for Jesus to return:

> And that ye study to be quiet, and to do your own business, and to work with your own hands, as we commanded you (1 Thessalonians 4:11).

> And we urge you, brothers, warn those who are idle, encourage the timid, help the weak, be patient with everyone (1 Thessalonians 5:14).

What is your new plan for waiting?

_____

_____

_____

_____

_____

_____

_____

_____

_____

_____

Dr. Jacqueline E. McCullough

The Purifying Moments

"Diamond Child"

There is a famous song, "Diamonds are a girl's best friend," but I am sure that this lyric is equally meaningful to some men. Diamonds are widely understood as symbols of status, beauty, esteem, and affection. Some people even become obsessed with them. This fascination with diamonds escaped me, as I was an exception to this rule. Not only were diamonds *not* my best friend, we hadn't even developed an acquaintance. For years, I treated not only diamonds, but also, jewelry in general, like a second-class citizen in the world of my attire. In comparison to other accessories, particularly shoes, jewelry was just not that important.

Then a few years ago, a well-meaning associate sold me a ring. The price seemed reasonable, but it never occurred to me to have it appraised. I didn't even bother to ask its value; I just assumed that I had purchased a diamond ring at a very reasonable price. One day, however, I showed off my ring to a group of female co-workers with much pride, hoping to receive compliments about the setting of the stone and the brilliance of the jewel. Instead, to my chagrin, one of the sisters passionately bellowed out, "This is not a diamond! This is zirconium!"

I was shocked. "Zirconium?" I said. "You mean this is not a real diamond ring?" I felt ignorant and embarrassed because I realized I did not know how to recognize diamonds.

To the casual observer, diamonds are everywhere. But to someone who has trained him or herself to discern a diamond, they know a real diamond is rare. The variation among these rare and costly stones is apparent to the person who has invested his or her time in distinguishing them.

From Dirt to Diamonds

With my new awareness that diamonds were more than just sparkling stones, my curiosity about gemstones began to exceed the mere recognition of diamonds in their glorious, faceted, final state. I wanted to know how a priceless gem comes from dirt and is transformed into a diamond. Let's go on a journey of discovering the process of transformation of what we call diamonds today. Come with me on the road that leads from the diamond mine, to the diamond refiner, to the diamond cutter, and ultimately, to the diamond wearer.

What process is entailed at each level of purification and transformation? As I set about getting a more sophisticated understanding of the process of refining diamonds, I began to discover some significant parallels to the spiritual process of refinement. Malachi 3:3 describes the spiritual process of refining,

"And he shall sit as a refiner and purifier of silver: and he shall purify the sons of Levi, and purge them as gold and silver, that they may offer unto the Lord an offering in righteousness."

This text refers to the coming of the Messiah, Jesus Christ, to the first century. It is He Who would cleanse the priesthood and establish His order in the earth. The priesthood was so corrupt and tainted that He came to set up a new covenant of holy priests and kings. This prophecy not only has a purifying, refining impact on the people of Israel and the religious hierarchy, but it also extends itself to all people.

As we journey through the stages of the purification and refinement of a diamond, we will be able to see from another perspective, the other side of "this." We may be better able to understand why the Holy Spirit is taking us through this journey of smelting and melting. Indeed, it is so that we can be transformed from dirt to a diamond. After all, the diamond was always a diamond, even in the belly of the earth. Therefore, we are always His children, even before the obvious refinement process. The Bible states that we were His before the foundation of the world. Therefore, no matter where we are in this process, we are His and always will be His *diamond child.*

Dr. Jacqueline E. McCullough

THE SEARCH FOR THE DIAMOND

The Process of Mining

Before diamonds become the dazzling, precious stones that we see in jewelry, they are hidden deep in the earth beneath layers of rock and sediment. As a result of indescribable heat and pressure, the diamond is formed. The stone itself is encased in a substance called "ore." *Webster's Dictionary* defines ore as "a naturally occurring mineral containing a valuable constituent (as metal) for which it is mined and worked."[8] Ore is similar to an egg white that holds a developing yolk. Kimberlite ore is said to be a type of volcanic rock best known for containing diamonds.[9] It is named after the town of Kimberley in South Africa,

---

[8] Webster, Noah. *An American Dictionary Of The English Language* (Springfield, MA: George & Chaples Merriam Publishers, 1850), http://1828.mshaffer.com/d/word/ore

[9] Balfour, Ian. "Famous Diamond" (1992).
http://www.amnh.org/exhibitions/diamonds/process.html

where the discovery of an 83.5-carat diamond in 1871 spawned a diamond rush.[10]

According to the Museum of American History, diamond mining and refinement can be broken down into a three-step process: *extraction, separation,* and *preparation.*[11] Let us examine the first step of the mining process — *extraction* — and draw out some similarities to our process of refinement when we are faced with a "this" situation.

The Process of Extraction

Diamonds are precious, and part of their value comes from the amount of difficulty associated with even getting the raw unfinished diamond to the surface. The diamond is hidden deep beneath the earth's surface and encased in mineral-rich ore. Two different practices for extraction are common in North America, open pit mining and the block caving method.[12]

Open pit mining is said to be the favored choice for many mining locations. In open pit mining, ore is removed with land movers and shovels, loaded into trucks and carried to the processing area.[13]

In the other method of mining, the block caving method, columns and tunnels are drilled into the Kimberlite. The tunnels are then lined with concrete with holes to catch the Kimberlite, which will be blasted by dynamite. The blasted ore falls into the tunnels and

---

[10] Dominguez, Vashi. http://www.diamondmanufacturers.co.uk/guidance-centre/glossary/glossary-k

[11] Janes, A. J. "A History of Diamond Sources in Africa: Part I" (1995). Gems & Gemology, 31: p 228-255

[12] Gorelick, L., and Gwinnett, A. J. (1988). http://www.amnh.org/exhibitions/diamonds/world.html

[13] http://academic.emporia.edu/abersusa/go340/students/laird/diamond3.html

is transported to a crusher by way of a pulley system. The ore is then transported from the crusher to the processing area.[14] Either method is complex and costly, requiring huge amounts of staff, time and machinery, not to mention extensive planning and logistical preparation.

It is such an extensive process necessary to extract, and even locate diamonds, that only the most committed and skilled miners seek them! The digging, drilling, and blasting require penetrating deeply into the ground until the ore is located. Depending on which process is used, the ore sometimes has to be removed by tremendous force, because it is not easily detached from its soil. How does that connect to our lives as we walk with the Lord? Consider the process by which God "mined" the first being. Genesis 1:27 states:

> "And the LORD God formed man of the dust of the ground, and breathed into his nostrils the breath of life; and man became a living soul."

The Hebrew word for dust is `aphar ("aw-fawr"), which translates "clay, earth or mud."[15] The Hebrew word for ground is 'adamah ("ad-aw-maw") which means "from the soil, redness, or earth."[16] But God did more than mere mining and refining; He loved His creation and gave him the breath of life. God not only extracted and

---

[14] Gorelick, L., and Gwinnett, A. J. (1988).
http://www.amnh.org/exhibitions/diamonds/world.html

[15] Baker, Warren; Carpenter, Eugene. *The Complete Word Study Dictionary Old Testament* (Chattanooga, TN: AMG Publishers, 2003). Hebrew word: *apar, STC# 6083, p. 857.*

[16] Baker, Warren; Carpenter, Eugene. *The Complete Word Study Dictionary Old Testament* (Chattanooga, TN: AMG Publishers, 2003) Hebrew word: *adamah, STC# 127, p. 17.*

formed, He created and made this rough diamond in the depth of the earth. Scripture tells us: "My frame was not hidden from you [LORD] when I was made in the secret place, when I was woven together in the depths of the earth" (Psalm 139:15). God extracted dust from the ground and masterfully created a "mud man" named Adam. This was the first "diamond child" in the "extraction" portion of the purifying process.

Much in the way that a diamond is encrusted with ore, the diamond child became encased in sin. Moreover, this diamond child was flawed. This same Adam was flawed and tarnished in his very nature by the sin of disobedience, which caused us, Adam's children, to inherit this flaw. With this spiritual flaw comes the fallen "Adamic nature."

We all know the story of Adam, and his helper and partner, Eve, and how the serpent deceived and tempted her. But the sin was not in the fact that she was tempted; her sin was in the fact that *she gave in to the temptation*, and in turn, so did Adam. They chose to be encrusted in the ore of their sin rather than be the perfect flawless diamonds God intended them to be. As a result of their sin, we are all trapped in our sinful nature from birth.

Each of us is extracted from the depth of the earth and formed by God: "For you created my inmost being; you knit me together in my mother's womb" (Psalm 139:13). God formed us knowing fully that we were "conceived in sin." Like Adam we are entirely covered in our sin, but as Christians, we are predestined to be diamonds. Jesus' death on the Cross was to separate us from our sinful "extracted state."

The extracted believer is covered by the "ore" of his fallen nature and trapped in our fallen state. For this cause, Jesus had to shed His blood on Calvary, which saved us from a downward spiral of sin and sinning and brought us into a new life in God through Jesus Christ. Every Christian today has endured the process of being extracted from the earth, covered in the dust and dirt of sin and separated from our sin by Jesus' precious blood.

The Separation State

In order for God to restore us, He had to bring forth another perfect, flawless diamond — One that would be the prototype for all others. That Gem, that "Pearl of great price" — is Jesus. Although God brought forth Jesus as a flawless gem, Jesus had to undergo the harshest possible "separation process" for us, so that we could be restored to God. Even though Jesus was not covered in the ore of sin, He had to be scourged and stripped. Because He is perfect, He withstood the harrowing process and came forth in victory and power.

There may be diamonds in the ore at the point when it is extracted, yet one would never know it without the intricate and very costly process that must take place in order for the diamond to be revealed.

The ore must still be further loosened, removed, and examined with precision and careful attention, so that nothing precious that is down in the midst of the rubble might be lost. Once we have been extracted with our "ore covering of sin," God begins the painstaking process of bringing forth our inner diamond.

The refinement is the separation of the diamonds from the rest of the worthless rock substance. The ore is put into a large funnel along with a heavy fluid and is then mixed, causing a rotation in the fluid. This process is much like panning for gold. The diamond is shaken in this mixture so that it can be successfully removed from those worthless minerals that are reducing its value.

As diamonds are heavier than the surrounding material, they tend to sink while the rest of the material rises to the top and is washed away. This is similar to the process of the refinement of precious metals! In the Book of Isaiah, the Messiah is described as being like "like a refiner's fire." The purity of His very presence removes our defilement. When subjected to heat and pressure, the dross and impurities in metal rise to the surface while the purified metal weighs more and has substance! Jesus is not only a Savior — He is a Refiner.

This separation can also be readily seen in the creation of man when God breathed His life into Adam's nostrils. This man of mud was now separated from dead things into a living being. Adam was a living creature with the God-given ability to function intelligently, emotionally and spiritually. God also gave Adam "free-will" to choose. Adam chose unwisely.

The process of separation only removes 99 percent of the impurities from the metal. To make the final refinement, the refiner has to place the metal under an x-ray machine to identify and remove the rest of the impurities.

This close scrutiny of an x-ray machine brings to mind the act of sanctification in the life of the believer. You see, Adam originally was without spot or blemish in his first creation state, but sin brought corruption to his body and soul. This corruption was transferred to the whole human race; therefore we had to be refined, washed, and cleansed by the blood of Jesus in order to have fellowship with God. The Bible declares, "In whom we have redemption through his blood, the forgiveness of sins, according to the riches of his grace" (Ephesians 1:7, KJV). When we first accept Christ, we are still mired in the "ore of sin."

Even after we have accepted Christ as our Savior, we have a certain percentage of dust, dirt, and carnality that has to be continually placed under the x-ray and microscope in order for the true gem of righteousness to be seen in our daily lives. Once the Holy Spirit draws us to Christ and we surrender our lives to His Lordship, we are His. For this reason, Christ sent His Spirit to continually transform us from a dusty existence into the state of a "diamond child." This means that we are moving daily to reflect Christ, with all His graces and power in our heart. This process of separation is called sanctification.

Sanctification is a theological term that is not often used by believers today. It may not even be part of the Church's vocabulary any more, but sanctification is a definite work of the Holy Spirit. What does this word really mean? Sanctification involves more than a mere moral reformation of character brought about by the power of the truth; it is the work of the Holy Spirit bringing our whole nature more and more under the influences of the new gracious principles implanted in the soul by God.

Easton's Bible Dictionary indicates that sanctification is the carrying on to perfection the work begun in regeneration, and it extends to the whole man (Romans 6:13; 2 Corinthians 4:6; Colossians 3:10; 1

John 4:7; 1 Corinthians 6:19).[17] It is the special office of the Holy Spirit in the plan of redemption to carry on this work (1 Corinthians 6:11; 2 Thessalonians 2:13). This means that every day, I have something that needs to be changed for the better. This "better'" is not what the world calls it; but this "better" is what is described in the Bible.

When I first came to this country from Jamaica, West Indies, I was very much alone, and terribly afraid. My dad worked during the day and my mother was a live-in baby nurse, who was away for three to six weeks per assignment. We lived in Harlem for a year, where I attended elementary school and The Greater St. John Pentecostal Church. These two institutions helped to assimilate me into the American culture. Yet the first year was extremely difficult and I cried every day.

I finally settled into church and gave my heart to the Lord at the age of 13. As I grew in Christ, I learned that I was saved, and fully sanctified, which led me to believe that I would not have any wrong thoughts, carnal desires, or negative feelings. I was overjoyed and riding on "cloud nine" in much the same way as a young bride sometimes does during the honeymoon phase of her marriage.

Honeymoons, however, do not last forever, and my honeymoon of "total sanctification" did not last forever. I could not drive all the earthly, carnal thoughts out of my mind and heart. I still had bouts of anger, words of unkindness, and feelings of rejection. This truly baffled me, because I thought that I was fully

---

[17] Easton, Matthew George. "Entry for 'Sanctification'". *Easton's Bible Dictionary*, Third Edition, Thomas Nelson, 1897. Public Domain.
<http://www.studylight.org/dic/ebd/view.cgi?number=T3212>.

clean and pure, without any desire to be sinful. Well, I was shocked to discover that there were parts of me that still reached for the world.

My family moved to Brooklyn a year later and I was attending a new school. I met quite a few children of Caribbean descent, and I gradually became a little more comfortable with my surroundings. The school had one of its annual parties, and I wanted to attend. I went with my cute pink dress, my newly processed hair, and a heart filled with excitement. I was going to have a social life! At the party, I talked with my friends, ate the sandwiches, drank the (non-alcoholic) fruit punch and danced my hips off! Yes, the tongue-talking, holy-rolling, Sunday school lover was eagerly, uncontrollably doing "The Twist." When it was over, I became extremely ashamed and walked quietly home, wondering why I behaved so out of character at the party. I kept asking myself, "Where was the vibrant churchgoer and Jesus proclaimer?" I prayed and cried the next day trying to get saved all over again. To my sad concern, this happened many times after that.

Later on in my walk with the Lord and through proper Bible teaching, I became aware of what was happening to me. I learned that I was and still am becoming like Christ daily; this knowledge has taken the burden off my back. I can walk in His life daily, knowing that His Spirit is working in me to bring me closer to His likeness. I will never be perfect until He comes again, but the glory in "this" is that I am being sanctified progressively, walking, living, and changing into a new creation through Christ. When we realize that we are a work in progress, we will not get stuck in the naïve need to be perfect in our own strength on our journey to the other side of "this"!

Preparation

The final purification stage for the diamond child is **preparation**. After the miner separates the diamond from the impurities, the diamond would still be unrecognizable. A rough diamond looks more like an ice chip, or an oddly shaped marble, than a glittering gem. The process of separation has only exposed the rough diamond, but the most significant visual refinement to the diamond happens in the preparation stage. There are criteria, which jewelers look for in a diamond after it has gone through the preparation process. This criterion is identified as the four C's of diamonds, which are: *Cut, Clarity, Color,* and *Carat.*[18] Let's examine the first two C's, the aspects of *Cut* and *Clarity,* specifically considering what is said about the quality of "Cut."

First, let us not confuse diamond "cut" with "shape." Shape refers to the general outward appearance of the diamond, (such as round, emerald, or pear). When a diamond jeweler says, "cut," that's a reference to the diamond's reflective qualities, not the shape.

Diamond cut is perhaps the most important of the four C's, so it is important to understand how this quality affects the properties and values of a diamond. When we talk about cut as a value factor, we're also talking about the proportions, symmetry and finish of a diamond. A good cut gives a diamond its *brilliance,*

---

[18] Eliot, George. "Gemological Institute of America." http://gia4cs.gia.edu/EN-US/index.htm

which is that brightness that seems to come from the very heart of a diamond. The angles and finish of any diamond are what determine its ability to handle light, which leads to brilliance.

The Process of Pruning

The thought of a "cut" often causes us to cringe. It suggests to the human mind pain, blood loss, and discomfort to the physical body. But we've all experienced a cut. We all have experienced the discomfort of a minor cut; whether it is a paper cut or a needle prick. Even generally pleasant experiences can lead to a cut. Picking roses from a garden, for example, can cause some discomfort when we come in contact with thorns.

There are deeper cuts, though. Sometimes a cut can be so deep that it completely cuts something away. The word that I associate with cuts is often used in the Bible as "pruning." This term is used by Jesus when He described us as fruit bearers in John 15:2:

> "Every branch in me that beareth not fruit he taketh away: and every branch that beareth fruit, he purgeth it, that it may bring forth more fruit."

Purging is another form of pruning. The word "purge" in the Greek is the word "kathairo," which is translated, in the *Strong's Concordance* "to cleanse; figuratively, to expiate."[19] This concept of pruning or cutting away causes the branch to become more fruitful. In a similar way, diamonds are pruned to remove rough

[19] Zodhiates, Spiros. *The Complete Word Study Dictionary New Testament* (Chattanooga, TN: AMG Publishers, 1993). Greek word: *kathairo, STC# 2508*, p. 792

surfaces and make them smooth and reflective. By pruning and purging, the diamond becomes smaller, but more valuable. The diamond that has the best cut shines with brilliance and increases significantly in value.

The right cut is critical. A diamond that is cut too shallow will not properly reflect light and will have a murky, dull and unreflective center. The diamond that is cut at too steep an angle will seem dull and lackluster. Only a master diamond cutter knows how to bring the most brilliance out of a diamond.

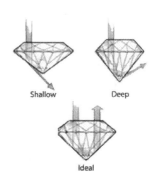

Have things been cut away from you spiritually? Have you lost a loved one, maybe in a way that felt like a cruel pruning? Or did you fail to achieve a lifelong dream? Did a piercing word from a friend challenge your beliefs? These are just some examples of the "cut." These cuts come into our lives to build up what is left, and to ultimately increase our value. How is it that a finished diamond can weigh less and yet be worth more than a rough diamond? This is simply because skill, force and pressure have been exerted on it. A master has worked on it and removed those things that prevented it from being brilliant and precious.

The same is true for us. That divorce was to remove something from you that was preventing you from shining. You can't find the right spouse if you are married to the wrong one. It had to be cut away at the right angle to allow you to shine without removing too much so that you would become murky and dull.

Likewise, you can't be promoted in your true calling if you are working the wrong "job." You had to get fired to remove the limitations and force you to get serious about dedicating yourself to your true vocation and calling. That slab of ego had to go so you could be humble enough to let God lead you to the work for which you are destined.

Cutting away and being separated from the familiar is very painful; but without it, you can never shine and bring forth your fruit. When we are placed on the other side of our "this," we will shine forth with such brightness out of our spirits, and substance from our experience, that it will surprise everyone. You are a diamond child who is being specially cut by the Master, so that you will produce great value.

Clarity

The other "C" is Clarity. A diamond's clarity refers to the presence of identifying characteristics on and within the stone. While most of these characteristics are inherent qualities of the rough diamond and have been present since the earliest stages of the crystal's growth below ground, a few are actually a result of the harsh stress that a diamond undergoes during the cutting process itself.

We are born with certain characteristics. The traits of our personalities that make us unique: our sense of humor, our intellectual capacity, and our emotional endurance are all the things which shape us from the beginning. Our clarity is determined from the start, but how our clarity is developed is part of the process.

Inclusions

If you think about the incredible amount of pressure it takes to create a diamond, it's no surprise that many diamonds have *inclusions* on the inside (clouds, feathers, included crystals) or surface blemishes (scratches, polish lines, extra facets). Inclusions are flaws either within the diamond itself or on the surface of a diamond which may or may not affect its overall appearance. Diamonds with no, or few, inclusions and blemishes are more highly valued than those with less clarity, not just because they are more pleasing to the eye, but also because they are rarer.

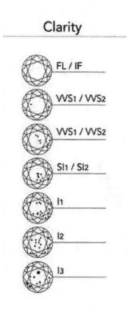

Clarity

FL / IF

VVS1 / VVS2

VVS1 / VVS2

SI1 / SI2

I1

I2

I3

Diamonds are graded for clarity under 10x loupe magnification. Grades range from "Flawless," which are diamonds that are completely free of blemishes and inclusions even under 10x magnifications; to "Included 3" diamonds, which have large, heavy blemishes and inclusions that are visible to the naked eye. Inclusions, then, are marks within the stone that have been included in the process of the diamond's formation. There are also things that we become attached to that are included in our lives.

Yet, when a master gem-cutter has fashioned it, the flaws, feathering, and blemishes can enhance the beauty of the stone. A masterful stonecutter can reduce or illuminate a flaw, not only in diamonds, but with any other material in life.

One of the most famous statues in history is Italian painter and sculptor Michelangelo's "David." But the background story of this masterpiece is not as well-known. The original block of marble from which the statue was carved was, in fact, ruined. A less experienced sculptor than Michelangelo had dug a long trench into the marble assuming that he could craft a freestanding figure. Due to his inexperience, the beautiful flawless white marble was cut nearly in half and threatened to give way under the sheer stress.

The stone was returned to the quarry where Michelangelo found it. In his masterful hands, the flaw in the stone was incorporated into the movement and meter of the sculpture. The next time you see an image of the famous statue of David, notice how most of the weight of his posture is on one hip and the corresponding shoulder is lower. Although this is a very natural and relaxed stance, it is extremely difficult to achieve with stone, especially an extremely hard stone.

The story of the flawed stone is mostly forgotten, but what remains is the beauty and grandeur of the statue. Michelangelo literally took the stone that had been rejected and made it into a masterpiece. Someone far more skilled is also available to shape us despite the flaws we acquire in the midst of "this." The key is our obedience and willingness to be reshaped by the Master.[20]

---

[20] Ripley, Elizabeth. "Michelangelo, 1475-1564." http://www.enotes.com/topics/michelangelo (March 2011).

Clarity and Character

I equate the clarity of a diamond to the character of an individual. This is the final word concerning your purification journey into becoming a "diamond child." Others often ignore a person's character flaws, especially when they have a lot of talent, skill, charisma, charm, fame and/or popularity. The superficial circumstances in which we encounter people are not a good indication of their character. Even seemingly good signs of character, like church attendance, can be deceptive.

The believer, who is living his or her faith daily, facing difficulty and undergoing hardship, must experience more than a church attendance and church affiliation to get pass the "this." As the actual diamond has inherent characteristics, so do we, but we have the Holy Spirit and His fruit abiding in our lives to enhance and reshape us in a more perfect way. Galatians 5:22-23 states, "But the fruit of the Spirit is love, joy, peace, patience, kindness, goodness, faithfulness, gentleness and self-control. Against such things there is no law."

The master jeweler seeks to identify any character flaw that can reduce the value of the diamond. He can easily damage a diamond because of pressure, which can leave scratches and blemishes. Sometimes these flaws are so small that it takes a microscopic view to discover the imperfections. This aspect of the diamond's formation is so similar to our "diamond childhood."

We are tossed about with winds of adversity and crushed with boulders of temptations. We are downtrodden with ill-fated relationships, and disillusioned with unfulfilled promises. These intentional or unintentional ministers of change can leave "inclusions," marks and scars. Yet Jesus, through His Word and by His Spirit, is a Great Physician and Master Healer. Like the miner, the processor, and the gem cutter, He refines us. But we are not just dead stones; we need Him to impart His life. He heals character flaws and brings our diamond light to a great shine.

2 Corinthians 5:17 is a wonderful text that brings to light our purification and transformation process. It says, "Therefore if any man be in Christ, he is a new creature: old things are passed away; behold, all things are become new" (KJV). The word "become" implies that something happens in the life of the individual that never happened before. It means that it is really new. Even before we transition on our journey to the other side of this, we can embrace this newness –pruning this, purging that and cleansing ourselves. It allows us to experience joy on the journey, and strength with each step that we take. We do not have to experience continual misery on our travels through life. As we embrace this process, we will complete our process of refinement and achieve our brilliant final state.

A Diamond Treasure in an Earthen Vessel

> "But we have this treasure in earthen vessels, that the excellency of the power may be of God, and not of us" (2 Corinthians 4:7).

So what have we learned on our travels through the diamond mine, the diamond refiner and the jeweler? Through this study, we see that there is something valuable in the earth and dust that we are, but it must be mined, developed, and worked. We must recognize that Christ within us, the Hope of glory, is the precious Diamond within our ore.

Yet, in order for the diamond within us to come forth, we must yield our lives to the work, process, and development of sanctification, so that we may reflect His glory, just as diamonds reflect the light at every turn and facet.

You are a "diamond child" who is going through all the needed processes to become more like the Father. Do not let the digging, the blasting, or the cutting blind your eyes to your becoming what God wants you to be. Yes, life has pain, sorrow, and disappointments, which I call the "this" in our lives. Look at what the diamond has to go through to reflect its value. Your brightness and your value are increasing because you are moving to the other side of your "this." Embrace it and rest in it today!

The Purifying Moments

Diamond Child

1. Read Chapter Two in its entirety. "According to the Museum of American History, diamond mining and refinement can be broken down into a three-step process: extraction, separation, and preparation." Which part of the process do you find yourself at this time in your life?

_____

_____

_____

_____

_____

_____

_____

_____

_____

_____

_____

_____

_____

_____

2. The process of separation removes 99% of the impurities from the metals. To conduct the final refinement, the refiner has to place the metal under an x-ray machine to identify and remove the rest of the impurities. Even after we have accepted Christ as our Savior, we have a certain percentage of dust, dirt, and carnality that has to be continually placed under the x-ray and microscope of the Holy Spirit in order for the true gem of righteousness to be seen in our daily lives. If you recognize that you are in this stage of the process, describe in detail your separation (also known as your sanctification) process.

_____

_____

_____

_____

_____

_____

_____

3. In what part of your sanctification process do you find yourself stuck? What have you done to change this?

_____

_____

_____

_____

4. John 15:2 says, "Every branch in me that beareth not fruit he taketh away: and every branch that beareth fruit, he purgeth it, that it may bring forth more fruit." Describe briefly your purging and pruning process.

_____

_____

_____

_____

_____

_____

_____

Spiritual Maturity

1. Are you mourning those things that the Lord has removed in the purging and pruning process? What is your plan to move forward from your disappointment? Be specific.

_____

_____

_____

_____

_____

_____

_____

2. When God's people endure the pressure in the preparation stage where we can encounter inclusions as stated in this chapter, it makes the diamond a very rare jewel. What would you say are some pressures you've endured that have made you a rare "diamond child"?

_____

_____

_____

_____

_____

_____

3. Can you identify any soul ties in your life that you may be struggling with?

_____

_____

_____

_____

4. What are some of the character flaws you have seen in your life? How have they caused you trouble in your everyday situations?

_____

_____

_____

_____

Personal Inventory

Have you embraced your process? Through this study, we see that there is something valuable in the earth and dust that we are; but it must be mined, it must be developed, and it must be worked. How are you yielding yourself to your process and development of sanctification, so as to reflect His glory?

> "But we have this treasure in earthen vessels, that the excellency of the power may be of God, and not of us" (2 Corinthians 4:7-8).

Using the above scripture, write a brief prayer that expresses the desire to embrace your process.

_____

_____

_____

_____

_____

_____

_____

_____

_____

_____

_____

The Other Side of This

The Removal of the Halo

In my experience, the churchgoing Christian often mistakes the outward appearance of "holiness" — that is, a certain kind of stoic behavior — for actual holiness. In my own personal and cultural experience, a woman was considered truly holy or saintly because her dress was well below her knees and her head was completely covered. In other religious settings, one may be considered saintly because he or she has a somber look and clutches their clasped hands to their breast. In the Roman Catholic Church, such outward piety is at least part of what is required for one to be canonized. Often, in artistic depictions, such exceptionally pious or righteous individuals are depicted with a halo. People well-versed in the various aspects of liturgy are sometimes even seen as holy.

All Things Angelic

Our modern society and culture is thoroughly enamored with the concept of the guardian angel. Angels are viewed as holy, but accessible. Scripture confirms this, "Are not all angels ministering spirits sent to serve those who will inherit salvation?" (Hebrews 1:14). Even in non-religious settings, angels are venerated and seen as very special. Shows like "Touched By An Angel," "Charlie's Angels," and even Oprah Winfrey's "Angel Network," declare a fascination with the concept of all things angelic. There are countless movies about angels and it is not unusual to find angels used to move the plot of a movie along. The idea of angelic presence and intervention gives humans a sense of comfort, safety, protection, and security. The concept of angels makes the spiritual realm seem safe and inviting. Even non-Christians seem willing to suspend their unbelief long enough to watch a movie or television show.

Generally angels are viewed as kind, good, and willing to help. For that reason, angels are considered to be special, holy, spiritual beings. This outward goodness is indicated by the angel's halo of goodness. Even in children's drawings, angels are depicted with a halo.

Understanding the Halo

Most dictionaries define a halo as a circle of light around the head of a saint in a religious painting.[21] It is an aura of glory imagined to surround somebody or something famous, sanctified or revered. According to some sources, a halo (also known as a nimbus, aureole, glory, or gloriole) is a ring of light that surrounds a person in art.[22] In astronomy, it is a circle around the

---

[21] Merriam-Webster Online Dictionary. Copyright © 2012 by Merriam-Webster, Incorporated. http://www.merriam-webster.com/dictionary/halo
[22] Ibid.

Moon or Sun caused by light refracting from ice crystals in the atmosphere.[23]

The word "nimbus" is translated from the Latin "cloud" or "glory."[24] It is the name given in sacred art to the disk or halo which encircles the head of the sacred personage who is represented.[25] The concept of the halo transcends our culture. It is used almost universally in ancient cultures ranging from China to Egypt and from Persia to Rome. The historical and archeological records we have indicate that the Etruscan, the Greek, and even the Roman used a halo in their artwork to depict those who were sanctified (i.e. set apart).

In Hellenistic Greek, Roman, as well as Buddhist and Christian sacred art, holy persons are often depicted with a halo in the form of a golden, yellow or white circular glow around the head. When the glow encircles the whole body, this type of halo is often called a "mandorla."[26] In these cultures, halos are often used in religious works to depict holy or sacred figures, but in various cultures and at various periods in time, halos have also been used to glorify images of rulers or heroes. With these definitions in mind, you can clearly see that the idea of the halo has to do with light, glory, sainthood and sacredness. It is a manifestation of innate goodness, virtue, or piety of the individual depicted.

---

[23] Bosiack, Kathy. "Astronomy." http://curious.astro.cornell.edu/question.php?number=79

[24] Merriam-Webster Online Dictionary. Copyright © 2012. http://www.merriam-webster.com/dictionary/nimbus

[25] Schiller, G. *Iconography of Christian Art, Vol. I.* London: Lund Humphries, 1971. http://www.newworldencyclopedia.org/entry/Halo

[26] Roccasalvo, Joan L., C.S.J. "Sacred Agriculture." http://www.sacredarchitecture.org/articles/called_to_beauty_through_iconography/

Light and Glory

In the Old Testament, this idea of brightness and glory is represented in the light which shone upon the face of Moses upon his return from Sinai in Exodus 34:29. As Moses descended from Mount Sinai with the two tablets of the Testimony in his hand, he did not know that the skin of his face shone because he had been with the Lord. "So when Aaron and all the sons of Israel saw Moses, behold, the skin of his face shone, and they were afraid to come near him" (NASV).

Moses emerged from the presence of the Lord with his face strikingly lit with the reflection of God's light and power. The word "shine" in the text is the Hebrew word, quaaranis, which means Moses was "horned."[27] Within biblical typology, the horn symbolizes strength, power, and might.

Therefore, the image of Moses clearly speaks of one who has received power, along with illumination, from God. In one very literal artistic interpretation of Moses, Michelangelo's huge and imposing statue in Rome, the artist depicts Moses with horns on his forehead.

Another great representation of light or glory is in the New Testament in the transfiguration of Christ. "And as he prayed, the fashion of his countenance was altered, and his raiment was white and glistering" (Luke 9:29, KJV). According to commentator David Brown of the famed Jamieson, Fausett and Brown commentary, "Putting all the accounts together, it would appear that the light shone, not upon Him from without, but out of Him from within: He was all irradiated: It was one blaze

---

[27] Baker, Warren; Carpenter, Eugene. *The Complete Word Study Dictionary Old Testament* (Chattanooga, TN: AMG Publishers, 2003). Hebrew word: *qaran, STC# 7160*, p. 1016.

of dazzling celestial glory; it was Himself glorified."[28] The word "glistering" in this passage means "radiant" or it "flashed forth as lightning," according to the Greek translation.[29] Can you imagine the face of our Lord Jesus filled with light and flashing forth with glory and power? What an awesome image!

These two passages of Scripture clearly reveal how the power of God's light, presence, and glory can be manifested through a human being. This light was not only external, but the outflow of an internal working of the heart of man. But what happens to the one who is illuminated? The Scripture clearly connotes that Moses' experience was so transforming that the murderer became an emancipator. In that instant, Moses was forever changed.

Even more miraculously, the glorious light of the transfiguration was just a hint and an intimation of the glory and splendor of our Lord Jesus Christ. In Jesus' transfiguration, what the disciples saw was the very image of God displaying inexplicable majesty. Oh, how the disciples must have been overwhelmingly awed by the brightness emanating from He Who is Light Himself!

The Origins of the Glory

In addition to the word "shine," another term associated with the halo is "glory." This is a commonly used word, which has been exploited in its use among churchgoers today. Most people inside or outside the

---

[28] Brown, David. *A Commentary On The Old & New Testaments by Robert Jamieson, A.R. Fausset & David Brown, Vol. III, Part I* (Grand Rapids, MI: William B. Eerdmans Publishing Company, 1978), p. 260.

[29] Zodhiates, Spiros. *The Complete Word Study Dictionary New Testament* (Chattanooga, TN: AMG Publishers, 1993), Greek word: *exastrapto, STC# 1823*, p. 601.

Church may see glory as a visible light, a great burst of spiritual energy or something too wonderful to describe. We may say, "Glory!" as we praise, but do we understand what we say? Let's examine what it really means in the original language.

The word "glory" in the Hebrew is *kabhodh*.[30] According to *The International Standard Bible Encyclopedia*:

> "The use and significance of kabhodh in the Old Testament and in Sirach: The fundamental idea of this root seems to be 'weight,' 'heaviness,' and hence, in its primary uses, it conveys the idea of some external, physical manifestation of dignity, preeminence or majesty. At least three uses may be distinguished: (1) It defines the wealth or other material possessions which give honor or distinction to a person; (2) the majesty, dignity, splendor, or honor of a person; (3) most important of all, it describes the form in which Jehovah (Yahweh) reveals Himself or is the sign and manifestation of His presence."[31]

When we say "glory" as Christians, are we really committing ourselves to the weight of His glory? Do we give glory to God in all three aspects of the definition? The word "glory" by this definition seems to be relational. It implies a hierarchy of greatness that must be acknowledged. The Greek word for "glory" is *doxa*, which means "splendor, brightness, magnificence,

---

[30] Bromile, Geoffrey W. *The International Standard Bible Encyclopedia.*
http://www.bibletools.org/index.cfm/fuseaction/Def.show/RTD/isbe/ID/3832/Glory.htm
[31] Ibid.

excellence, preeminence, dignity, grace."[32] Both definitions of glory have an internal and an external component; a spiritual and an earthly manifestation. "Glory" implies a relationship in which someone is transformed, acknowledged, or "graced" by God.

The Halo Moment

I remember my first sermon, which is commonly referred to as a "trial sermon." I was 19 years old, worshipping at the St. John Pentecostal Church, in Harlem, New York, under the leadership of the late Bishop Lenora Smith, a woman of prayer, devotion and faith. She was a very graceful but powerful influence in my life, and anointed me at the age of 16, during a Sunday morning service.

She often anointed the young people and spoke words of wisdom and guidance into their lives. I stood at the back of the line that Sunday morning, very much afraid and hesitant. I directed other young people to get in line ahead of me, hoping that I would be forgotten.

You may wonder why I was reticent to receive my anointing. An anointing is special event. It is recognition that God has a purpose for us. I was looking beyond receiving recognition in front of my peers. Bishop Smith was such a powerful woman who operated in the gifts of the Spirit, particularly in the word of knowledge and prophecy. I had seen her prophesy over other young people, and I was in awe of her. For me, it was like when an angel of God appears. I was in awe, but it also struck fear in me.

---

[32] Thayer, Joseph. *Greek English Lexicon of the New Testament* (Chicago IL: Harper & Brothers, 1989), Greek word: *doxa*, p. 155.

When angels brought messages to people in the Bible, there was a similar reaction. When the angel appeared to Mary or Joseph, they experienced fear in the presence of the angel. Perhaps, spiritually, I was sensing that Bishop Smith was going to say or do something that would make things very different.

When God came to Moses on the mountain, Moses took off his shoes on holy ground — knowing that he was in God's presence and about to be transformed. My reticence came from my sense of anticipation; I knew something very weighty was about to happen. I wasn't expecting anything spooky or eerie. In fact, I was hearing Bishop Smith's prophetic voice. I was hearing what she was saying to other young people who were there with me, and I knew, in my soul, that it had power. It was what I heard her saying that made me aware that she was speaking to them about their lives. What she was saying was both awesome and important for the future.

I didn't know what she was going to say to me, but I knew it would be my "rhema" Word from the Lord. A "rhema" is a Word that is brought to a person's attention or remembrance in the time of need. *Strong's Exhaustive Concordance* defines it as "an utterance, that which is or has been uttered by the living voice, [a] thing spoken."[33] The rhema is intentional and fitted for your situation at the time. It is a personal, situational Word brought forth by the Holy Spirit that brings life and breaks spiritual yokes. It's a personal spoken and fitted Word. The "rhema" Word is not spooky; it flows

---

[33] Blue Letter Bible. "Dictionary and Word Search for *rhēma (Strong's 4487)*". Blue Letter Bible. 1996-2012. < http:// www.blueletterbible.org/lang/lexicon/lexicon.cfm?Strongs=G4487&t=KJV >

from the written, *logos* Word. It is logical, safe and based on Scripture.

Well, needless to say, I received a double dose for my reticence. She anointed me with much oil on my head, which ran down onto my face. Then she spoke loudly with much emphasis and passion, which penetrated my spirit and captivated my heart. She declared, "You are called to preach the Gospel to many people. You will travel far and near and you will be based in New York." I ran into the arms of my mother and wept profusely. I cried as an act of worship. I was humbled by her words and I felt broken before the Lord. The Spirit of the Lord had penetrated my soul, and I felt the way Mary felt when she prayed the Magnificat in Luke 1:46, "My soul doth magnify the Lord...."

The light of God shone inside me and illuminated places of darkness that had been shrouded in innocence and ignorance. From that point on, it dictated so many of my choices. In the days that followed that moment of anointing, the Lord continued to affirm my path and my prayer. I didn't become exceptionally pious and begin to walk around with my hands clasped as if in a monastery. Like David tending his sheep after the prophet Samuel's anointing, I went back to my life with my parents. But, that moment, that encounter with God, has always stayed fresh in my mind and heart.

It was a "halo" moment. From that moment on, my life was never the same. I had to live with the conscious knowledge of those words. They gave me an awareness that my life was going to be different. My future was wrapped up in the Lord. My experience with the Lord was confrontational, much like that of Saul on the Damascus road. It changed who I was and affected everything about me. David had his "halo moment," Saul had his "halo moment," and Mary had her "halo moment." These "halo moments" are a sign of maturing faith. Halo moments, like a "rhema" Word, are about remembrance. We have halo moments so we can remember when and where we first believed. Every Christian should have a transformative "halo moment" and quickly be able to recall the date to mind. A "halo moment" will light the path to the other side of "this."

Taking Off the Halo

Just as there are real halos, there are also false ones. We can make icons or idols out of worldly things, placing a halo on something and hoping we can make it glow. We can glorify fame or wealth or status. The Bible tells us: "For where your treasure is, there your heart will be also" (Matthew 6:21). It is possible to treasure material things so much that we glorify them. They take our hearts. We place a halo on our "stuff," rather than on the things and experiences that God has for us.

How do we take off our halo? We do it by acknowledging Christ as first in our lives. Three years after my "halo moment," I stood before Bishop Smith, the church leaders, my family, and most intimidating, my peers, and preached my first message. I was terrified. However, despite my fear, I preached, and that message has remained in my spirit to this day. It was entitled, "Consider the Lilies," and was taken from Luke 12:22-32:

"And He said to His disciples, "For this reason I say to you, do not worry about your life, as to what you will eat; nor for your body, as to what you will put on. For life is more than food, and the body more than clothing. Consider the ravens, for they neither sow nor reap; they have no storeroom nor barn, and yet God feeds them; how much more valuable you are than the birds! And which of you by worrying can add a single hour to his life's span? If then you cannot do even a very little thing, why do you worry about other matters?

Consider the lilies, how they grow: they neither toil nor spin; but I tell you, not even Solomon in all his glory clothed himself like one of these. But if God so clothes the grass in the field, which is alive today and tomorrow is thrown into the furnace, how much more will He clothe you? You men of little faith! And do not seek what you will eat and what you will drink, and do not keep worrying. For all these things the nations of the world eagerly seek; but your Father knows that you need these things. But seek His kingdom, and these things will be added to you. Do not be afraid, little flock, for your Father has chosen gladly to give you the kingdom."

This particular passage is a source of deep comfort to care-worn believers. Anyone who discovers this text in Scripture is sure to have a refreshing of their soul that can be likened to finding an oasis in a burning desert. In my sermon, I found that the soul of the text was putting God first. This text reorders our selfish priorities, instructing us to seek the things of His Kingdom first. Then, and only then, will He add what we need to our lives so we can flourish. That sermon has taken me on a journey toward removing my own glory, my own halo, my own design, and my own will, and giving my life fully to God. It is only at this point that we all can shine for Him and become a radiant reflection of His presence in the earth.

What does your halo consist of? Is it fear? Is it pride? Is it security? Is it arrogance? Please sit for a minute and consider if you are really living to please God or merely living to please yourself. The manifestation of where the glory or the weight of your power comes from is readily apparent in your priorities. What you are glorifying is seen in your choices, relationships, goals, ambitions, attitude, and activities.

The Halo of Relationships

Relationships can be very revealing when it comes to "halo-wearing." Just as Mary, Martha and Lazarus humbled themselves to Jesus and surrendered their glory to Him, we connect and relate in similar ways. God created people to have connection and communication. Humanly, we were created to affect each other in all areas of our lives.

I remember in the early part of my traveling ministry, I visited Bermuda quite often. I still have some very strong relationships there. The island is so beautiful; the ocean, teal green; the people, kind and friendly; and the food, fresh and delicious. As in many areas around the world, there are certain nuances in their vernacular and local dialect. While speaking, many Bermudians punctuate and add emphasis to their conversations and dialogue with the phrase "Umum." I am from Jamaica, and when we are speaking, we often inject our language with the term "ee" to punctuate our phrases. Well, after spending some time on the Island of Bermuda, I traded in my "ee" for their "Umum." How did this happen so quickly? My friendship and association pulled me into their world and my speech patterns began to assimilate. My love for my friends was evident in my speech, whether for negative or positive.

What about difficult relationships? What about a relationship we feel trapped in? Can taking off the halo of self help us in difficult relationships? Aren't we told that lack of self-esteem and self-worth are what lead us into destructive/difficult relationships? The Bible never talks about "self-esteem." Christ must be esteemed in us. We can't have self-esteem and "Christ-esteem" at the same time. Nothing we have can be held up to Christ to be esteemed.

Remember, Adam's sin separated us from God. We have no ability to redeem ourselves from that sin. God loves us despite our sin. God loves us so much, He chose to pay the price for our sin and free us. If we love and esteem Christ for His sacrifice, we are no longer separated from God and can share in His power. God has power to heal, to renew, to rebuild, and, even, to resurrect.

What if the difficult relationship is a marriage, or an employer, or a parent, or even a child? In the same way that relationships can build us up, and purify us, relationships can also tear us down and contaminate us. Relationships that contaminate us can cause us to feel insecure and injured. The Lord is using those experiences of broken and damaged relationships to bring us closer to Him. Robert S. McGee writes:

"When we trust Christ and experience new life, forgiveness and love, our lives will begin to change. Still, regeneration does not affect an instantaneous change in the full realm of our performance. We will still continue to stumble and fall at times, but the Scripture clearly instructs us to choose to act in ways that reflect our new lives and values in Christ."[34]

Self will fail us, people will fail us. That's why we're constantly in pain. Christ can and will renew us if we are willing. We have the truest form of self-esteem when the one who we *want to be esteemed is Christ. Our true value is in who Christ is.* "For in Him we live and move and have our being" (Acts 17:28). Our identity and value is in Him. We must allow our value system to be wholly centered in Him.

When we have Christ-centered esteem, relationships, especially difficult relationships, become transformed. Because we put Christ first and are living to please Him, we are not overly concerned with acceptance or rejection. We are also less sensitive to insults and opinions, because we are measuring our relationship(s) by godly, and not worldly, standards. We can show compassion where we once showed anger; we can set boundaries where we once felt ashamed; and we can feel free to do what is right and not what is popular.

How do we stay in relationships with people who refuse to get along? "If it is possible, as far as it depends on you, live at peace with everyone" (Romans 12:18).

---

[34] McGee, Robert. *The Search for Significance* (Nashville, Tennessee: W Publishing Group, 1990), p. 114.

That is a beautifully clear statement of the standard. Do everything you can do to be kind and loving. But, when it is not possible to get along and the person you are trying to relate to wants to destroy you, safety is the priority. For example, in Acts 14:19, when Paul was teaching in Lystra, the citizens of that city conspired to stone him, and he had to be taken away to safety.

But, if there isn't abuse in the relationship, then we are required by Scripture not just to honor, but to love — that is, *agape*. The onus is on us to love, not on the person to accept our love. Can we hold on to our conviction to behave true to the character which Christ built up in us? "This" relationship may depend on our ability to do just that. If we can hold onto "this" relationship, we are assured a closer walk with Jesus.

Outward or Inward Holiness?

Scripture states in Ephesians 2:8-10, "For it is by grace you have been saved, through faith — and this not from yourselves, it is the gift of God, not by works, so that no one can boast. For we are God's workmanship, created in Christ Jesus to do good works, which God prepared in advance for us to do."

We are saved, rescued, and delivered from the darkness of sin into the brightness of Christ's light, based on His sacrifice for us on Calvary. There is nothing you or I could have done to change our minds towards God. It was strictly an act of love from Christ Jesus, and this act of love changes our lives continually.

The truth of the matter is, if we will be honest, that we, as humans, are prone to taking the credit. We are raised in a society that takes pride in human effort, human intellectualism, human accomplishment and humanistic values. When you or I meet someone, they more often ask about what we do than about who or how we are. Self-absorption and self-centeredness have created a stronghold in our churches.

A "spiritual–stronghold" derives from the notion of a fortress, or a fortified place. It is built to keep something from coming in and to prevent anyone from going out. It's a strong wall tower or castle. Biblical Jericho was a stronghold, for the walls were built to prevent invaders, including the ancient Israelites, from coming in and conquering (Joshua 6:1). A stronghold cannot be shaken, moved, or penetrated. People depend on the stronghold to protect their lives in times of trouble. It can be likened to a mindset which cannot be changed. In a good way, our faith can be a stronghold that protects us from the whims and ideologies of the world. For example, in Zechariah 9:12, it says, "Turn ye to the stronghold, ye prisoners of hope."

In that particular passage of Scripture, it means turn to the help of your fortress for your strength, which is God. That is a positive aspect of the stronghold of a mindset. A stronghold is also where we go to renew our strength, but if that stronghold is not enduring, we can suffer harm when our stronghold collapses.

Where do you go to get your thoughts strengthened and your mindset affirmed? When our mindset comes from someplace other than the Lord, we can be trapped in a stifling place. Strongholds of imagination are particularly damaging. In 2 Corinthians 10:5, it says, "We demolish arguments and every pretension that sets itself up against the knowledge of God, and we take captive every thought to make it obedient to Christ." The enemy sets up such strongholds to destroy our faith.

Trapped in a stronghold of self-absorption, we can become obsessively concerned with material comfort and gain. Such self-centeredness can justify un-Christian behaviors and attitudes that we aren't even aware of, because we are justified by "self" and not by "God's Grace." Sadly, the very Gospel that we preach often has more to do with what we can get, how high we can climb and how great we can become. We reduce God to a celestial ATM rather than a Way-maker for those who "earnestly seek Him." It seldom has to do with the walk of holiness that was prescribed by Jesus in the Bible.

We are powerless and frustrated with God, yet we have abandoned His ways. It is as if we went to the doctor, got diagnosed, received a prescription for medicine and therapy that could heal us, and refused to fill the prescription or seek the therapy. And then, we blame the doctor and call him a "quack." We have left the true meaning of the Christian life and are doing our own thing, even in the Church. How very sad that our self-absorption has made us self-deceived.

Our flesh wants the glory, the credit, and the acknowledgement for any manifestation of power, goodness and blessings. We cover ourselves in our own "glory cloud" (to use the popular language), which clearly beclouds the sovereignty of God in our affairs.

When Mary, the sister of Martha and Lazarus, anointed Jesus with her hair (John 12:3); she was taking off her glory and giving Jesus the honor that He deserves. Many of us grew-up being told that a "woman's hair is her glory." The old saints considered long hair a beautiful, natural covering that was given to women. Mary, probably had long hair, humbled herself and worshipped the Lord, trusting that He would love and protect her for this gesture. It was not acceptable for a woman in her culture to let her hair down in public. She ran the risk of removing the halo of tradition and culture to reveal her undying love and devotion for Jesus.

The idea of glory for the Bible-believing Christian cannot be centered upon both God and self. What do we have, that we have not gotten from the Lord? All of our achievements, exploits and feats have been because of Him. He alone is worthy, meaning He only has the weight, the power, and the strength to execute His purpose in our lives.

Every one of us has an example of something that failed because we were functioning in our own strength. Whether it was a failed marriage or a degree in something we never used or an attempt to "keep up with the Joneses," we have all failed at something because God was not acknowledged. There are numerous examples in Scripture of the Armies of Israel going out to battle without consulting the Lord, or in defiance of His Word, only to be routed and defeated by the enemy. How many times have we watched someone (enemy or friend) painstakingly build something, gloating in a momentary victory, only to have all their efforts come crashing down because God was not with them?

It is like the wise and the foolish builder in Matthew 7:24-27. Both men built sturdy houses, yet only one house withstood the storm. That house was built on a Rock foundation, which is obedience to Christ.

The Bible-believing Christian must be able to lay down self, and take off the halo of self in order to access the glory of God.

And Have Not Love

But what about people who are self-sacrificing, but are obsessed with works? Or those who are always eager to take care of others and do "good works," but who are angry and resentful of others at the same time? One of the most famous passages in Scripture comes from the 13th Chapter of 1 Corinthians. A person who is fundamentally resentful of others is not showing love, no matter how much they work or give of themselves. The passage goes so far as to say, "If I give up my body to be burned." What greater sacrifice could one make? Yet, it would not be enough of a sacrifice if it were done without love.

Even great kindnesses performed without love are empty, according to Scripture. Certainly things done grudgingly do not meet that standard. In Scripture, it says plainly, "Each man should decide in his heart, not reluctantly or under compulsion, for God loves a cheerful giver" (2 Cor. 9:7b). The Lord wants us to be courageous in our hearts and resolve to give not only money, but love, so that He in turn can love us.
What if we know someone will disappoint us? Can't we protect ourselves and set limits? That is not love. Love does not give with a stipulation or an expectation. People who give grudgingly share something in common with people who want to justify themselves by their good deeds — the same need to set boundaries and grudgingly show love. What does the 13th Chapter of First Corinthians require of us really? Well, if we look

carefully, the passage speaks only to the one who is to love; it does not require the person who receives the love to accept it. That is the power of love — that love is not the position of a coward. To truly love, we must love courageously as Christ did, with confidence and faith. Christ loved us even when we were not willing to accept His love. "This" is not remotely as terrible as what He suffered for us; He loved us even when we could not accept it.

The Halo of Kindness (Agape)

If you want to set boundaries, let "kindness" be your measure. True kindness seeks what is best for the other person despite what they may want, or what you may want to give. Do not mistake being "used" for love as license for being abused; you do not have to be a doormat for someone. Those types of relationships are, at best, abusive, and, at worst, they are an even more sinister dance-partner of abuse, "enabling." We call many things love that are not love; they are often abuse, manipulation, and enabling. Watch what you are giving as love, it may not be love. It is amazing how people who are unkind want all the kindness in the world. Such people know kindness when they receive it, but they would never come near it otherwise.

Kindness searches for an opportunity to do good for a person. Find ways of being kind, even if others are unkind to you. Kindness is not just giving you what you want. For example, if I know you like pink lollipops and have a mouth full of cavities, giving you a lollipop that you like is not for your good. Kindness is not just giving to make me feel good. I like to see you smile because it makes me feel good. But is it good for you? Kindness is taking the opportunity to do what is good and beneficial for another. If giving you pink lollipop is not good for you, I shouldn't give it to you. I am being kind by withholding lollipops because I want you to have teeth! Again, kindness is taking the opportunity to do what is good. Anything else is the sentimentality of a soap opera, but true kindness will take me to eternity. Church will cease, marriage will cease, prayer will cease, but kindness will take me into eternity.

There are eternal values. My kindness will take me to heaven. When you do it right, kindness is your ticket to be with God. No unkind person will be able to be with the Lord. Are we being loving? Are we being loved? Are we showing kindness and receiving it? For the most part, people are not aware of this kind of love, but now you know. How do you know? God has kindness for you. He is sending kindness and patience into your life right now. As difficult as it may be to accept, love is someone unconditionally helping you to become what God wants you to become. Kindness, showing and receiving it, will not only get you through "this"; the Halo of Kindness will usher you into eternity.

The Halo of Godly Relationship

As people on earth, we cannot escape the emotional, intellectual, physical, and spiritual influences that we have on each other. God intended it to be that way from the very beginning. The Bible declares in Genesis 2:18, "And the Lord God said, It is not good that the man should be alone; I will make a helper for him." In the original language, the word "good" means "favorable, best, delightful, beneficial"[35]; therefore, we understand that it is not favorable, best or delightful for man, or anyone, to be alone. "Alone" means "separate, or apart[36] as a branch is separated from the vine." Life sustains life and people are meant to receive support from each other.

Our choices of friends, mates, associates and comrades reflect what "halo" we are wearing. The glory, the light of God, can be readily seen or obscured by the people to whom we attach ourselves. You may say that is not necessarily true, because you can be around people and still maintain your identity and individuality. Yes, we all have our individuality or personality, but not separate and apart from our connection with the human family. The Bible speaks of the apostles in Acts 4:13:

> "Now when they beheld the boldness of Peter and John, and had perceived that they were unlearned and ignorant men, they marveled; and they took knowledge of them, that they had been with Jesus" (KJV).

This passage serves as a backdrop for the healing of the lame man at the gate called Beautiful through the ministry of Peter and John. This man went away leaping and praising God to the point that the people were amazed. This miracle gave Peter an opportunity to

---

[35] Baker, Warren; Carpenter, Eugene. *The Complete Word Study Dictionary Old Testament* (Chattanooga, TN: AMG Publishers, 2003), Hebrew word: *tob - STC# 2896*, pp. 399-400.

[36] Baker, Warren; Carpenter, Eugene. *The Complete Word Study Dictionary Old Testament* (Chattanooga, TN: AMG Publishers, 2003), Hebrew word: *bad - STC# 905*, p. 118.

preach about the resurrected Christ and many believed. The Jewish rulers, however, who arrested Peter and John, were amazed that Peter spoke so boldly, convincingly, and eloquently about his faith in Christ Jesus.

They were confounded because these men didn't have rabbinical education and were not schooled in the religious schools of Hillel or Shammai. Yet, they spoke clearly and profoundly about the Messiah, making plain the prophets' foretelling of Jesus. Their speech and understanding had the mark of personal acquaintance, association, and intimacy. The rulers noted that the way they spoke openly revealed that these men had been with Jesus. The Spirit of the resurrected Christ, the teachings of His principles, and the power of His love influenced these men to the point that it was readily seen by others, even their enemies, that Jesus was their intimate Friend and Teacher.

We are influenced by people through personal contacts, family relations, books, media and friendships. These influences will either bring us to Christ or draw us away from Him. You might wonder how television or a classmate might have enough influence to affect our Christian walk. But the shadow of unhealthy attachments will certainly keep us from His glory and light. You and I are being courted and wooed by every doctrine and worldly influence in dozens of subtle and not-so-subtle ways. These influences are manifested in the form of relationships, media, arts, and our choice of activities.

We must make Him our chief joy and primary love in order to wear His "halo." Only when we embrace the light of God through fellowship in prayer, Bible reading, and healthy church bonding, can we then take off our "halo" of self, our external form of brightness, and truly glow from within, knowing we have the fullness of Christ's glory and power.

Peter, a crude fisherman, became a great prolific preacher, teacher and writer. He was transformed into someone who changed his world and he became a representative of the Kingdom of God because he wore the "halo" of Christ on the inside. He did not allow his limitations, inexperience, failures or the many aspects of "this" to keep him from walking in the light and boldness of God's power. The change in Peter was so evident that others were greatly affected, not by Peter himself, but by the glorious light that shone through him.

Let us lift off the "halos" of tradition, fear, rebellion, and indifference and embrace the light, power, and love of God within our hearts. Whatever "this" may be in your life today, chances are it will be something else tomorrow. Taking off our "halos" and seeking God first will supply us with what we need to get through "this." As a result, peace, grace, and mercy will exude from our lives in such a way that others will know that we have made it to the other side of "this."

The Removal of the Halo

Understanding the Glory of God
Read Chapter 3 in its entirety. Both definitions of glory have an internal and an external component; a spiritual and an earthly manifestation. It implies a relationship in which someone is transformed, acknowledged, or "graced" by God. In reference to your relationship with the Lord, how would you describe His earthly manifestation in your life? What spiritual changes have been manifesting in your spiritual life? Has anyone else noticed these changes?

_____

_____

_____

_____

_____

_____

The Halo Moments
1. List any "halo moments" you may have had in your life. How have they changed you?

_____

_____

_____

2. What have been some false "halo moments" in your life? Have there been things that you have placed halos on hoping to make something glow?

_____

_____

_____

_____

_____

_____

Spiritual Maturity: Taking Off the Halo

1. Can you acknowledge your selfish priorities? How have you put God first in your life in these areas?

_____

_____

_____

_____

2. What does your halo consist of?

_____

_____

_____

_____

_____

_____

3. Consider for a minute if you have been living to please God or merely living to please yourself? Write your reflections!

_____

_____

_____

_____

_____

_____

4. Taking off the halo of self helps us in difficult relationships. Are there any relationships that you feel trapped in? How has pride crept into the situation? What have been some of your selfish demands?

_____

_____

_____

_____

_____

_____

_____

_____

5. Relationships can build us up, and purify us; they can also tear us down and contaminate us. How have some of your difficult relationships brought you closer to Him?

_____

_____

_____

_____

_____

_____

_____

_____

6. Romans 12:18 says, "If it is possible, as far as it depends on you, live at peace with everyone." What are some of the insults and opinions that you hear from the difficult people in your life? What is your plan to live at peace with these people in your life? In what way will you show them biblical love?

_____

_____

_____

_____

_____

7. Safety is priority! How do you plan to rid yourself of those relationships that are toxic to your relationship with the Lord?

_____

_____

_____

_____

_____

_____

_____

Personal Inventory: Outward or Inward Holiness?

1. If we are honest and really want change, it is crucial to see where we are erring. Sometimes we are obsessively concerned with material comfort and gain because we believe these things define us. They say to others that we are of a certain status and block the grace of God in our lives. In what ways do you see yourself taking the credit?

_____

_____

_____

_____

_____

2. How loving have you been in your giving? What expectations or stipulations have been attached to your giving? Have you expected the other person to receive your love, and feel rejected when they don't?

_____

_____

_____

_____

_____

_____

_____

_____

3. If you want to set boundaries, let "kindness" be your measure. True kindness seeks what is best for the other person despite what they may want, or what you may want to give. Again we are not talking about being a doormat or a relationship that is abusive, manipulative or enabling. How will your new boundaries look? Be specific.

_____

_____

_____

_____

_____

_____

Dr. Jacqueline E. McCullough

The Winding Valley

How many times have you heard a sermon that talks about your "valley experience?" Valleys usually suggest hard times, difficult days, and sleepless nights. Everyone that is born into this world has and will have times of adversity. It is impossible to live on this planet without difficulty, and, I suppose, even if we move to Mars, we would still have unforeseen hardship.

Princes and beggars alike experience loss, disappointment and hardship. But what does hardship mean? Why do these things happen to us? Is hardship a sign of weak faith, empty spirituality or a backsliding heart? It seems to be human nature to search for the meaning of adversity.

There are times when we bring difficulties upon ourselves. For example, if we have a particular bill and we squander the money on a frivolous desire, then we will suffer the consequences. The consequence may be an eviction notice on the door or having the lights turned off in the house. It takes introspection and maturity to realize that there are times when we cause our own negative consequences. Irresponsible action will bring on suffering and a journey through the valley. There are, however, circumstances beyond our control, which do not reflect a weak faith or distrust in God's divine love. Sometimes the stronger our faith, the greater the test!

The Nature of the Valley

What is a valley? Geologists define a valley (frequently called a vale) as "a hollow sweep of ground between two, more or less, parallel ridges of high land."[37] "Vale" is the poetic or provincial form sometimes favored by theologians. It is usually the case that the center of a valley is occupied by a stream which forms as water drains down from the high ground on either side. The term "valley" is distinguished from other geological terms, which are, more or less, closely related to a valley in form of a "glen," "ravine," "gorge," or "dell." All these terms are used to describe a depression in the earth's surface which is, at once, more abrupt and yet also smaller than a valley.

With this definition in mind, we can see that a valley is a depressed area physically, which figuratively could also correspond to a low period in one's life. Is that where you are now? Your perspective can determine a lot about your time in the valley. If you are in a valley right now, you probably need to journey with me through the valley and see whether you can define your valley differently.

A couple of years ago I preached a sermon entitled "Another Level of Anointing." This sermon was taken from Psalm 23. The core and strength of the

---

[37]Merriam-Webster Online Dictionary, Copyright © 2012 by Merriam-Webster, Incorporated
http://www.merriam-webster.com/dictionary/valley

sermon for me was in looking at David's valley experience. The preparation for this sermon took me to Phillip Keller's classic works, which includes an exhaustive study of the 23rd Psalm in "A Shepherd Looks at Psalm 23." Keller broadened my understanding of the necessity of the valley in order to appreciate the mountain experience. He states:

> "Both in Palestine and on our western sheep ranches, this division of the year is common practice. Most of the efficient sheep men endeavor to take their flocks onto distant summer ranges during summer. This often entails long "drives." The sheep move along slowly, feeding as they go, gradually working their way up the mountains behind the receding snow. By the late summer they are well up on the remote alpine meadows above timberline."[38]

So, we see that various seasons determine what kind of "shepherding" is called for. Because of their need for tender grass and fresh water, the sheep must be guided in a certain direction, depending on the season. In summer, the heat tends to compromise the quality of the grass that the sheep feed on. By the mid-summer because of the heat, it is necessary to go higher up the mountain for cooler temperatures and greener, fresher grass.

Regrettably, the summer season does not last forever. With the unavoidable return of cooler weather,

---

[38] Keller, Phillip. *A Shepherd looks at Psalm 23* (Grand Rapids, MI: Zondervan, 1996), p.68

and with the change of season, the need emerges to redirect sheep. Keller goes on to say,

> "With the approach of autumn, early snow settles on the highest ridges, relentlessly forcing the flock to withdraw back down to lower elevations. Finally, toward the end of the year as fall passes, the sheep are driven home to the ranch headquarters where they will spend the winter."[39]

The convergence of autumn and the change of seasons necessitate a change of journey. The shepherd's ultimate job is to guide, protect and provide for the sheep. The job of finding provision has to do, mostly, with finding the best food and water in each season. Keller states:

> "In the Christian life we often speak of wanting 'to move onto higher ground with God.' How are we to live above the lowlands of life? We want to get beyond the common crowd, to enter a more intimate walk with God. We speak of mountaintop experiences and we envy those who have ascended the heights and entered into this more sublime sort of life. Often we get an erroneous idea about how this takes place. It is as though we imagined we could be 'air lifted' onto higher ground. On the rough trail of the Christian life this is not so. As with the ordinary sheep management, so with God's people, one

---

[39] Ibid, p.69

only gains higher ground by climbing through the valleys. Every mountain has its valleys. Its sides are scarred by deep ravines and gulches and draws. And the best route to the top is always along these valleys."[40]

The trip to the mountaintop has a season. In the proper season, the valley is a safe route out of the low lands and up to higher ground. The ascent can be really difficult, but the reward of being up high with the beautiful green valley stretching out beneath makes the trip worthwhile. But seasons change. When it is winter, the mountains are snowcapped and the vegetation has gone; this leaves the land barren of vegetation, and so there is no food for the sheep. The mountain can then become a place of desolation, barrenness and death during the winter months. The only place to find food, water, and life is in the valley. The season of remaining in the valley can be a cold and limiting one. Resources are spare in winter, even in the valley.

The Valley of Safety

But there is provision. God provides for us when we have to wait for spring in the valley. In the valley, we can be protected from the storms of winter, the icy conditions, and even the occasional avalanche. When the mountaintop is out of season, the valley doesn't seem so bad, if we can recognize that our safety, provision, and protection are most available in the valley.

---

[40] Keller, Phillip. *A Shepherd looks at Psalm 23* (Grand Rapids, MI: Zondervan, 1996), p.69

Here are a couple of examples of safe, but stressful, valleys. Many of us, who have gone through the rigors of higher education and who have graduated, know that graduation is a mountaintop experience, but that first job can be a valley! Filled with ambition and good intentions, we train for years, only to find ourselves working an entry-level job for low pay. The very ambitious among us go to graduate school and live modestly while going further into debt. Talk about a valley! But the time spent making these sacrifices is also a wonderful time. We form real and lasting friendships, because we don't have the resources to impress our friends. Friends have to like us for who and what we are. We learn to improvise, sacrifice and be self-disciplined. God provides for us while we are down there, and He is preparing us for our mountaintop experience; but for a time, we are stuck in the valley.

For some of us, the safe valley comes after a divorce or the death of a spouse. It is tempting after a relationship fails or is lost to just run out and look for any experience that "feels" like it will take us higher and out of the valley of our despair. But, for those of us with patience, who are willing to trust in God, that valley can be a place where we learn about self-control and humility.

Alone with God in the Valley

Most frightening of all, we can learn who we are and whose we are. After a divorce, many people are eager to jump into another relationship because they are afraid to be alone. Or some of us become workaholics to avoid our pain. We need the distraction and excitement of "new love" or obsessive "work" to keep us from the emotionally overwhelming recognition of loss. There is a reason the marriage ended, and we sometimes feel we need distractions to avoid that knowledge. After the death of a spouse, one may feel depressed, lonely and vulnerable, which could lead to the desperate desire to connect with anyone who can fill the void of emptiness.

When we are alone with God, we are forced to reckon with the real reason the marriage failed — not just what he or she did wrong, but our role — what we did. Maybe, despite our good intentions, the relationship was wrong for us from the beginning. In that valley, alone with God, grappling with our tarnished self-images and beat-up egos, we are humbled, but maturing; regretful, but renewing; down-trodden, but fulfilled. In that winter valley, the Lover of our souls is crafting us into soul-mates. When we are ready, He will give us that rare gem of self-forgiveness, which reflects and illuminates our lives with forgiveness toward others. In the valley of the loss of a spouse, Jesus gives comfort like none other.

It is there that the steadfast love of the Lord never ceases. It is there that grief does not become our master. Jesus died for our sins, and if we love Him, we don't have to keep self-punishing. We can start rebuilding our lives on the foundation of Jesus, crucified, ascended, resurrected. Whether we ever remarry or not, that season in the valley alone with Him will make us whole where we are deeply broken. With this in mind, you should now begin to see that where you are is the best place to find the life of Christ, because to move could result in spiritual and emotional desolation and death. To remain, just for a season, will insure you a newness of life and an understanding that guarantees that you will never be the same.

Moving Through the Valley

The valley is, by definition, a place we must move through. The word "valley" in Psalm 23:5 is the word "ge" (pronounced *gay* in the Hebrew), which means "to flow."[41] It is a deep narrow ravine with a (winter or perennial) stream at the bottom either between hills (like the Ge-Hinnom at Jerusalem) or through an open plain (as along the Mediterranean or in Moab). Picture the steep foreboding walls that line the side of the valley, and the harrowing and treacherous terrain at the bottom. It is difficult to traverse a place like that. This does not sound like a pleasant place to dwell. As a matter of fact, it is a valley like this that is termed in the text as the "valley of the shadow of death." The darkest aspects of death are evident in this place. It is not just the terrifying specter of death, but death's chilling shadow that blots out all the lights, except for one — the Light of the World.

So, it is clear why the important point of the text concerning this valley is that you pass through this valley and not dwell there. Just flow with God! While we are in this valley, there is such a heavy darkness that it can be felt; yet our travail is a temporary situation, and not a long-lasting one. With God, even in the presence of death, we pass through to the other side of the valley in safety. However near the shadow may come, God is right there with us.

---

[41] Baker, Warren; Carpenter, Eugene. *The Complete Word Study Dictionary Old Testament* (Chattanooga, TN: AMG Publishers, 2003), Hebrew word: "*gay*," *STC# 1516*, pp. 198-199.

We are intended to be pilgrims in our valleys. God has already made a way; we just have to follow it, which should encourage us to walk through and not become paralyzed.

David in the Valley

The valley suggests a place of danger, which is as dark and gloomy as the grave. You may be at such a place, where the tunnel of the shadow has completely obscured the light of hope and change. The medieval Talmudic scholar Rashi believes that this Psalm describes David's experience in the wilderness of Ziph, where he was betrayed and hunted by Saul in 1 Samuel 23:19-29.[42]

David, who was a brave and valiant warrior, was reduced to hiding from Saul, his master and his spiritual father, in the Wilderness of Ziph, which was a barren desert region. This is one of the most trying and perilous times of David's fugitive life. He is being pursued by a mentally disturbed king, whose quest was to destroy him. Yet, David, who had slain the lion, the bear and even the giant, had now met with an "unkillable" adversary. Saul, despite his madness, was still the Lord's anointed. Imagine how much self-control it took for David to flee in humiliation from Saul, when he could so easily have killed him and seized the throne. After all, he, David, was anointed and ordained to be king at a specified point in Israel's history by the Prophet Samuel — the same one who anointed Saul.

Didn't David have the better "new and improved" anointing? Didn't it just make sense that David should

---

[42] Guber, Mayer I. *Rashi's Commentary on Psalms*, Brill Reference Library of Judaism, 2004, pp. 264-265.

strike Saul down to underscore how crazy Saul had become? But David was a seasoned sojourner in the valley. He knew that nothing good would come from striking down the anointed of God. David had spent enough time alone with God. David was patient and respectful of God. Despite the hardship he and his men suffered, David chose to flee when he could so easily have fought and won. It must have seemed like a cruel joke to David in 1 Samuel 24 when Saul was discovered resting unguarded in the cave where David and his men were hiding. But David persevered. He did not allow his men to harm Saul. How dark and confusing the valley must have seemed at that moment. Was God testing him? Was Satan tempting him? Did it matter? Did his men think he was a wimp? Or did they think he was just as crazy as Saul?

It is hard to even imagine the faith, self-restraint, and the genuine fear of God that David must have had. In this day and age, parishioners openly critique the sermon and the order of worship, and they eagerly spread rumors and gossip about the men and women of God without a second thought. Moreover, the electronic media feeds us a steady diet of rumors, allegations, and mistakes made by clergy. Family members and whole congregations are not spared such humiliation by the press.

And yet, just while we are uncritically watching another pastor being savaged on television, we forget the wisdom of David, who would not harm God's anointed in the least way — even when Saul may have deserved it. We lament and grumble, asking God why we are still in the valley, without checking how we are treating God's anointed. Like some modern-day pastors and evangelists, Saul was in the wrong, yet David still respected him. David feared and loved God more than he wanted the throne of Israel, and more than he wanted status or luxury or even material comfort. David was submitted and obedient; God brought David out of the valley.

David knew God was passing him through his valley of death threats. What are you passing through, that is causing you to doubt and withdraw from God's Word and promise? Your Chief Shepherd, Who is Christ the Lord, knows the dangers, tests, and temptations in your valley. Keller says:

> "The shepherd knows from past experience that predators like coyotes, bears, wolves or cougars can take cover in these broken cliffs and from their vantage point prey on his flock. He knows these valleys can be subject to sudden storms and flash floods that send wails of water rampaging down the slopes. There could be rock slides, mud or snow avalanches and a dozen other natural disasters that would destroy or injure his sheep. But in spite of such hazards, he also knows that this is still the best way to take his flock to the high country. He spares himself no pains or trouble or time to keep an eye out for any danger that might develop."[43]

You cannot make it to the mountaintop circumventing the valley. The valley is the only way to get to the mountain. Before one of my favorite uncles (lovingly known as "Uncle Chappy") died, my mother

---

[43] Keller, Phillip. *A Shepherd Looks at Psalm 23* (Grand Rapids, MI: Zondervan, 1996), pg. 73.

and I used to visit him in the hills of Clarendon, in Jamaica, West Indies. I dreaded going up the hill, but the hill started from the lowland. It was a gradual climb onto narrow, winding roads. The more the roads wound, the higher we climbed. It was a consuming experience. On the one hand, I was tired out by the effort it took to climb, but on the other hand, the vistas were stunningly beautiful. All my senses, my heart, and my soul were fully taken up in the experience. Similarly, we move from the "lowland" to the "high land" of our lives, because valley experiences are not necessarily permanent.

The valley of trial and testing is an all-consuming experience. It takes all our strength to undergo the testing, tempting, limiting and stretching required to come through. God knows what we are made of, but He wants us to know it too. Most importantly, God wants us to love and trust Him.

The Valley of Judgment

But there is another valley that we all must travail—the Valley of Judgment. It is our human condition to sin. In Romans it says: "All have sinned and fallen short of the glory of God" (Romans 3:23). Please note that it does not say "some have fallen short," it says "all!" In John's epistle, it says, "If we say we have no sin, we deceive ourselves and the truth is not in us" (1 John 1:8).

Perhaps it will come as a surprise to you, but the same King David who was so obedient, self-controlled, faithful, and submitted to God in the desert strongholds, openly lusted after another man's wife. He not only lusted after her, he schemed to have her brought to him, seduced her and then got her pregnant. As if that were not enough, he had her husband murdered in an effort to prevent the sin from being discovered. How shockingly out of character! But not really, because David was human.

How could someone who was so close to God, who served as an example to his people, someone who was brilliant and who walked in the favor of God, just lose control and sin in such a vile way? David had his pick of beautiful women. He had wealth, power, and influence beyond imagining, and if he had asked God for more, David would have been given more. How could he do such a thing?

How could a famous pastor or evangelist do such a thing? Isn't that the question we ask ourselves so often? But the questioning can get a lot closer to home. Sometimes we are forced to ask: *How could my spouse do such a thing? How could my boss do that to me? How could my own child betray me that way?* And the most frightening question of all: *How could I have done such a thing?*

Come with me to the dark valley of those who have fallen into sin and let's examine the truth about sin. We are all sinners because our "first father," Adam, sinned. Through him, sin entered us. It's as if sin was not in our DNA and when Adam sinned, it became part of our genetic code. We are born with it, just as we are born with a certain eye color and a particular hair texture. Sin is in us. Sin also separates us from the righteousness of God.

Sin is always lying dormant in us, and we know from the Bible that sin can enter into us. "Then dipping the piece of bread, he gave it to Judas Iscariot, son of

Simon. As soon as Judas took the bread, Satan entered into him" (John 13:26). But we are not just passive agents; sin doesn't just overtake us like a bandit. We plot, plan, and intend to be in sin — it's our nature. We want separation from God. We stray far into the darkened valley of sin thinking we can escape Him and have our own way. But God wants us; He loves us and was willing to sacrifice His Son to be reunited with us when we were still deep in our intentional sin — deep in the valley.

In Jeremiah 2:13, the Judean people, the people of David's heritage, had abandoned God. Historically Judah was having conflict with God and was seeking an alliance with Egypt, a nation of idolaters. In trying to change their God, they were changing their glory. Their sin was far worse than David's. Idolatry is the mother of all sin; it is fundamental shifting away from what is righteous — God.

When Judah strayed away from God, He continued to woo Judah; He followed Judah. But the Judean people persisted in their sin; they had become corrupt and evil. When we are evil, our relationship with God is not intact. The Judeans forsook their Source of righteousness and intentionally entered the valley of sin. God had been a Source of spiritual "Water" for them, which was like the clean water of a mountain spring. Spring water does not rely on rainfall, it is able to keep itself supplied; the melting snow, the underwater aquifer, the "unseen" water sources, provide a constant supply. A spring bubbles up from the ground.

The Judeans of Jeremiah's time were like David when he became inflamed with lust for Bathsheba; they planned to forsake the Lord. But why would a man *plan* to leave the comfort and direction of God? Why would a man *plan* to betray his Savior? Why would a people *plan* to stray? Why? Because once you have experienced the greatness of God in your life, you can't leave Him without a plan! It was the Southern Kingdom's calculated plan to step away from God and ally with Egypt because they couldn't believe that God could rescue them.

Likewise, David couldn't believe that God would give him more than he could imagine. At the time of Christ's betrayal, Judas, having witnessed the miracles, signs and wonders, couldn't believe that Jesus is the Son of God. Self, and then Satan, plotted together to forsake God. They had apostatized. That is what forsaking is — apostatizing, which is turning away from revealed truth; it is turning from truth we already know.

We all want to escape God. So, like David, Judas, and the Judean people, you and I have all tried to escape God by entering the Valley of Sin. We mistakenly believed there is freedom and satisfaction in the Valley of Sin, but the Valley of Sin isn't even a valley, it's actually a narrow pass that leads to a dark and terrible place — the Valley of Judgment.

Biblical scholars agree that David wrote Psalm 51 during a time of deep contrition, probably after he sinned with Bathsheba. This psalm, which is 19 verses long, begins with these six verses:

> "Have mercy on me, O God, according to your unfailing love; according to your great compassion blot out my transgressions. Wash away all my iniquity and cleanse me from my sin. For I know my transgressions, and my sin is

always before me. Against you, you only, have I sinned and done what is evil in your sight; so you are right in your verdict and justified when you judge. Surely I was sinful at birth, sinful from the time my mother conceived me. Yet you desired faithfulness even in the womb; you taught me wisdom in that secret place" (Psalm 51:1-6).

The author of these words is clearly in the valley. He is so lost that he is no longer even trying to help himself. He is asking for mercy from the burden of his sin, and sin's close companion, guilt, which is pressing in on him like the walls of a dark, rocky crevice. There is no turning back and undoing his sin; there is no more trying to cover it up. The Valley of Sin is a trap. The narrow path leading along between the two rocky unforgiving walls named "Guilt" and "Regret" just keeps getting narrower as we continue, in vain, to try to carry on as if nothing has happened. All the while, our sin just keeps getting heavier to bear.

David's sin was like a lurid soap opera. After he seduced and impregnated the wife of one of his leading military commanders, Uriah the Hittite, David had Uriah killed by ordering that he was to be abandoned during a battle with the Philistines. But God was watching, and the man of God, Nathan the seer, accused David to his face of "using the sword of the Philistines," to destroy Uriah.

David is guilt-stricken, but tragedy soon strikes him. Not only does Bathsheba's baby die of a mysterious fever, but David's son Amnon succumbs to a fever of lust and rapes his virgin sister, Tamar. Then David's most beautiful and beloved son, Absalom, betrays him by murdering his older brother, Amnon, and ends up attempting to dethrone his father, cohabiting with his father's concubines in full view of all Israel. Eventually, the tragic and rebellious Absalom is killed and David's kingdom is restored, but not before David is forced to flee for his life from Absalom's wrath and murderous hatred. Even by today's standards, that is a risqué and sordid story. But more significantly, it is a dark and terrible valley that David had to cross because of his sin.

So how did David get out of the Valley of Sin? He confessed, "Against thee, thee only, have I sinned, and done this evil in thy sight: that thou mightiest be justified when thou speakest, and be clear when thou judgest" (Psalm 51:4, KJV). David is clear that despite all the people he hurt and even killed, the only one he really sinned against is God. This doesn't mean the people he hurt were not important. It means that the people he hurt matter a great deal to God — the One he sinned against. When David confessed and repented, David passed through his sin into the Valley of Judgment.

In the Valley of Judgment, God not only leads us on a path of forgiveness, He introduces us to the real meaning of our sin nature. "Surely I was sinful at birth, sinful from the time my mother conceived me" (Psalm 51:5). Our sin has been with and a part of us from the time we were conceived! We are helpless to do anything about it. David wanted mercy; he was disgusted with his sin and knew there was nothing he could do to undo his sin. He couldn't go back in time; he couldn't change himself. He needed mercy: "Have mercy on me, O God, according to your unfailing love; according to your great compassion blot out my transgressions. Wash away all my iniquity and cleanse me from my sin" (Psalm 51:1).

God gave David wisdom in that Valley of Judgment to understand that God is merciful and just. He wasn't just going to get away with what he did, but God was going to show him mercy. God led David to understand that even though he had been conceived in sin, it was God's original intention that we would be "faithful." God always succeeds with His intentions: "Yet you desired faithfulness even in the womb; you taught me wisdom in that secret place" (Psalm 51:6).

Scripture says that Abraham's "faithfulness" was credited to him as "righteousness." So although we can never be righteous before God, God will give us credit for being faithful as though we were righteous. David came to that knowledge in God's "secret place": that Valley of Judgment, which becomes a place of transformation. It is in the Valley of Judgment that we meet a merciful God Who, with mercies and loving kindness, will guide us through all the travails that await us because of our sins. We have to get real; we have to confess. We need God's mercy and forgiveness to get through "this."

Dropped into the Valley

Sometimes we just find ourselves in the valley. The Bible says that Job was "perfect"; yet he found himself being used as God's instrument for showing Satan that he did not have greater control over man than God does.

Job went from being rich and contented one day to being poor, sick, childless, covered in painful scabs, and scorned the next. His wife stayed with him, although through her attitude, some pastors have argued that a spouse is one of the devil's most potent ways of tormenting us. (But that is a discussion for another time!) Imagine how shocked poor Job was as he grieved in the ash heap mere days after disaster struck his life.

I am also reminded of my earlier days when I frequented my favorite theme park, Coney Island, in Brooklyn, New York. Every teenager in my circle went to Coney Island to enjoy the most thrilling ride, "The Cyclone." It is still the most sought after attraction at Coney Island today. Its wild highs and lows, with the gradual ascent and the wildly sudden plunge, are truly a metaphor of life. Sometimes in life, we are headed up one minute, and dropped down into the depth the next.

For instance, almost every adult in our society has lost a job we enjoyed or left a job we hated. Sometimes a loss is sudden. We aren't prepared for it. It can come as a great shock. But take comfort in the reality that God was not taken by surprise. He knew this would happen, and more importantly, He has already worked out the complete solution. God is unchanging and solid as a rock. The Lord tells us in Scripture, "'I know the plans I have for you,' declares the Lord, 'plans to prosper you, and not to harm you, plans to give you hope and a future'" (Jeremiah 29:11). But you might be wondering, if God has already handled everything, what is my role? Our job is like David's; we have to get to know what God requires. If knowing God is our priority, we will discover not only how to manage our own lives, we will find out about the many blessings God has in store for us.

Those sudden drops of the rollercoaster, plunging us into a deep dive, are intended to heighten our anxiety, anticipation and apprehension while we are gradually rising to the top. Once I got off the Cyclone, I felt the physical and emotional effects of being on a rollercoaster. I was giddy and exhilarated, yet glad to be on solid ground.

It is like the experience of resting on Christ the solid Rock after having fallen suddenly into the valley. You may be going through your valley feeling like you are on a rollercoaster; but take heart, because you will experience the solid comfort of the Lord.

There is no need for comfort if you are doing well, feeling fine, and living it up. The comfort of the Lord will not be expended unnecessarily. God is a wise economist because He does not waste Himself, as a deceased friend of mine always said. He gives comfort to the grieving, lonely heart; He gives joy to the sorrowful soul, and He gives hope to the dejected spirit. If you are well, you do not need a physician, as Jesus wisely pointed out to the Jewish leaders of His time: "…It is not the healthy who need a doctor, but the sick. I have not come to call the righteous, but sinners to repentance" (Luke 5:31-32). He, therefore, will give comfort and guidance to us as we go through our valley experience, because that is when we need it.

The Rod and the Staff

The rod is used by the shepherd to care for and comfort the sheep. Keller says:

> "The rod speaks, therefore, of the spoken Word, the expressed intent, the extended activity of God's mind and will in dealing with men. It

implies the authority of divinity. It carries with it the convicting power and irrefutable impact of 'Thus saith the Lord.' ...There is a second dimension which the rod is used by the shepherd for the welfare of his sheep — namely that of discipline. If anything, the club is used for this purpose perhaps more than any other...It is the Word of God that comes swiftly to our hearts, that comes with surprising suddenness to correct and reprove us when we go astray...Finally, the shepherd's rod is an instrument of protection, both for himself, and his sheep, when they are in danger. It is used both as a defense and a deterrent against anything that would attack."[44]

Keller declares that the staff represents the Holy Spirit and it operates in three ways:

"The first of these lies in drawing the sheep together into an intimate relationship...The staff is also used for guiding the sheep...Another common occurrence was to find sheep stuck fast in labyrinths of wild roses or brambles where they had pushed in to find a few stray mouthfuls of green grass. Soon the thorns were so hooked in their wool they could not possibly pull free, tug as they might. Only the use of a staff could free them from their entanglement."[45]

---

[44] Keller, Phillip. *A Shepherd Looks at Psalm 23* (Grand Rapids, MI: Zondervan, 1996), pg. 82.

[45] Ibid, pp. 84-86.

Please note that the comfort here comes from the rod, which is the Hebrew word *shebet* (shay'-bet).[46] It is used to correct or discipline the sheep. Our winding valleys are often places of discipline, not punishment.

God is not cruelly whipping us into shape, but showing us a better way to live, and guiding us into the way that is pleasing in His sight. If He does not correct us, we will be thoroughly destroyed as we walk through the dangerous ravines of this earthly life. Determined to do it "my way," we can so easily be crushed by sin, and lost in our own iniquity.

The Hebrew word for "staff" is *mish'en* (mish-ane'); or *mish'an* (mish-awn'); which is defined as "a support" (concretely), or (figuratively) "a protector or sustenance." In the King James Version, the word is translated a "stay."[47]

The combination of rod and staff in the hand of a loving Shepherd affords us immeasurable comfort. The idea is that the Word of God and the Holy Spirit will protect, correct and guide each of us through the valley. This support and guidance will bring me comfort, which means my mind will be changed from fear to faith; from sorrow to joy; from discouragement to encouragement. Being corrected and protected go hand in hand. Even when we are suddenly snatched into something terrible and unspeakable, there is a strong and stable staff that will rescue, correct and protect us.

As I write this, I am reminded of the morning I went to the hospital to view my father's body. I had just

[46] Baker, Warren; Carpenter, Eugene. *The Complete Word Study Dictionary Old Testament* (Chattanooga, TN: AMG Publishers, 2003), Hebrew word: *masenah, STC# 4938*, p. 687.

[47] Ibid.

visited him the night before and he was jovial and spicy with his words, as usual. We had a great conversation and I went home with the intention of meeting him the next day for his minor surgery. Suddenly, unexpectedly, I was called at 3:00 a.m. on Monday morning to rush to the hospital, because he was dying. When I got there, he had crossed over to the other side. The attendant who had been with him told me that he laid his head on her shoulder and went to sleep. He was guided gently over to the other side of "this."

Even though I know that my Dad is with the Lord, the grief was unbearable. I was a "Daddy's girl" and was blessed to have him alive up to the age of 90. Yet, I was overwhelmed with sadness and despair.

As I left the emergency room exit to come home, I felt as if my mind was about to fly out of my head. I wanted to run upstairs to the hospital room and grab my father's body and bring him home with me. However, in an instance, I felt the grace of God lift my sunken heart and brace me up for my ride home. I believe that the Holy Spirit, as a staff, guided me through that dark valley, and is still guiding me whenever I sense the loss of my dear father.

I am sure that you have your own testimonies about the guiding hand, the caring touch and the gentle voice of the Good Shepherd as you experience your winding valley and your challenging path. If you don't have a testimony yet, you will. As the valleys open up before you, remember that the Good Shepherd is with you. He knows how to get you safely through. You will pass through "this" because His rod and staff will comfort you.

The Winding Valley

Defining the Valley Experiences

After reading Chapter 4, answer the following questions:

1. List some of the valley situations in your life at this time; are they circumstances that were caused by your frivolous desires or negligent behavior? What are the consequences of your frivolity or negligence?

_____

_____

_____

_____

_____

_____

_____

_____

_____

_____

_____

_____

_____

2. A basic definition for a valley is "a depressed area physically," which figuratively could also correspond to a low period in one's life.   What is your perspective concerning your legitimate valley experiences? Do you see where your perspective needs to change?

_____

_____

_____

_____

_____

_____

_____

_____

_____

_____

3. In what areas of your life are you avoiding walking through the valley to get to higher ground?

_____

_____

_____

_____

_____

4. Are you in a relationship that has failed (a marriage, a best friend, a boss, etc.)?

_____

_____

_____

_____

_____

_____

5. In what ways are you becoming stagnant or paralyzed in your valley experiences?

_____

_____

_____

_____

_____

_____

_____

_____

_____

_____

_____

The Valley of Judgment

6. Does your valley experience include the judgment of
God upon your life because you are critical regarding
leadership in the Church? What are some of the things
you tell yourself that makes you believe that it is
acceptable to criticize leadership? What are your plans
to cease?

_____

_____

_____

_____

_____

_____

7. David knew God was passing him through his valley
of death threats. What are you passing through, that is
causing you to doubt and withdraw from God's Word
and promise?

_____

_____

_____

_____

_____

_____

Spiritual Maturity

8. What plans have you deliberately calculated as a result of struggling in your faith? How are you trying to escape God?

_____

_____

_____

_____

_____

_____

_____

_____

9. The people in your situations matter a great deal to God; like David in Psalm 51, how many people have you found that you are hurting?

_____

_____

_____

_____

_____

_____

_____

10. Do you recognize that you have sinned against God? In what way have you sinned against God?

_____

_____

_____

_____

_____

_____

Dropped into the Valley

11. In what ways are you feeling the comfort of God? Describe the fear that is now faith and the sorrow that is now joy.

_____

_____

_____

_____

_____

_____

_____

_____

_____

Personal Inventory
Write a brief testimony about God's guiding hand, His caring touch and gentle voice in your winding valley and challenging path.

_____

_____

_____

_____

_____

_____

_____

_____

_____

_____

_____

_____

The Other Side of This

Flipping the Needlepoint

I love needlepoint! I just don't have the time to indulge in this delightful pleasure the way I desire. My mother, Evangelist Keturah Phillips, taught me how to sew at a very early age. In Jamaica, West Indies, where I received my formative years of education, I learned how to enhance this skill. Despite having become skilled at a number of crafts, I still prefer needlepoint and crochet to knitting.

Some of you might be unfamiliar with these various forms of handicrafts. Needlepoint might invoke images of a loom and other antiques, but needlepoint is as current a hobby as it ever was; numerous magazines and websites are devoted to helping enthusiasts improve their skills. Let's explore a brief description of the history of needlepoint.

Needlework, or embroidery, has been around almost as long as clothing itself. Samples of embroidery have been found in Egyptian tombs, on ancient Maori costumes from New Zealand, and on medieval church vestments. Embroidery includes anything you can do with a needle and yarn or thread on almost any type of material. Western culture tends to link needlework to women, but, originally, it was a task performed by men who spent years mastering the craft.

You may be in the midst of a period in your life that is not making sense. Your bewilderment may cause you to wonder what needlepoint has to do with this period in your life. Well, let's look at the craft itself and see if the designing of the craft of embroidery can compare to the intricate design of your life. The hand of the Supreme Creator, the Lord God, crafted your life. But how are His workings, weavings and interconnections with us reflected through needlepoint?

For more insight, I went to the American Needlepoint Guild's website. It was here I discovered that they described this art as "embroidery." So let us look closely at the art of embroidery. One dictionary defines *embroidery* as "the art of working raised and ornamental designs in threads of silk, wool, cotton, gold, silver, and other material, upon any woven fabric, leather, paper, etc., with needle."[48]

Another dictionary simply declares embroidery as "elaboration or embellishment, to produce or form in needlework."[49] Still another states, "Embroidery is an art which consists of enriching a foundation by working on it with a needle and colored silks, cottons, wools, etc., in floral, geometric, or figure designs."[50] As we review these definitions, the key words to consider in understanding embroidery are "create" and "design."

---

[48] Alderson, Chottie. *"American Needlepoint Guild,"* 1997,
http://www.needlepoint.org/Archives/00 03/history-i.php.
[49] *Ibid.*

[50] *Ibid.*

Fearfully & Wonderfully Made

The notion of "design" takes me back to when I first started ministering across the United States in the early nineties, when I did many seminars for women. The first seminar I did was based on Psalm 139 and was entitled "Fearfully and Wonderfully Made." This Scripture has ministered to many hearts and I am sure it will to yours.

According to the scholars, the jury is still out as to whether this psalm is a Davidic psalm or a description of someone who was a captive in Babylon. Whether David was the author or not, we can glean that whoever wrote this psalm had a vision of God's creative power in his life. In spite of the writer's challenging experience, he decided to look at himself as a human tapestry intricately woven by a designing hand —the Hand of God. If this is a psalm of David, then we understand his connection to this psalm, having experienced much depreciation and dehumanization during the various exiles of his life.

If the Psalmist is in exile in Babylon, then we can conclude that the author experienced feelings of loneliness and alienation. The known Psalmist of the Babylonian exile declares in another Psalm, namely Psalm 137:3,

> "For there they that carried us away captive required of us a song; and they that wasted us required of us mirth, saying, Sing us one of the songs of Zion. How shall we sing the Lord's song in a strange land?"

The separation from their land had caused them to become depressed. If you have ever been homesick, you know the great pain the exiles experienced. But even if you've never moved away from home, you surely know about loss. Loss is being exiled from the persons or things that you love. How many times have you become depressed in the midst of your exile experience? Then you can understand what the Psalmist experienced in the midst of his loneliness and feelings of isolation and grief. Whether in exile or fleeing for his life, the Psalmist searched for and found an understanding of his most fundamental being.

Despite feelings of grief, despair and disillusionment, a new declaration was made in Psalm 139:14: "I will praise thee; for I am fearfully and wonderfully made: marvelous are thy works; and that my soul knoweth right well." The writer decides to praise God because the tapestry of the magnificent crafting of his being was worth celebrating. The word "praise" in the Hebrew is *yadah*, which means, "to give thanks, to boast and to confess."[51] We can see what the writer is grateful for, but what is the writer confessing? He is rightly confessing the greatness of God.

The writer realizes that he is the eternal handiwork of a Master Designer, which no one could imitate or duplicate. Therefore, he chose to give thanks for his human existence, even in the midst of difficulty. What was this writer's realization? He had the realization and understood intimately that he was "fearfully and wonderfully made." Barnes' commentary

---

[51] Baker, Warren; Carpenter, Eugene. *The Complete Word Study Dictionary Old Testament* (Chattanooga, TN: AMG Publishers, 2003), Heb.: *yadah, STC# 3034*, pp. 419.

captures, for me, the essence of the Psalmist's illumination:

> "The word rendered 'fearfully' means properly 'fearful things'; things suited to produce fear or reverence. The word rendered 'wonderfully made' means properly to distinguish or to separate. The literal translation of this-as near as can be given-would be, 'I am distinguished by fearful things'; that is, by things in my creation which are suited to inspire awe. I am distinguished among thy works by things, which tend to exalt my ideas of God, and to fill my soul with reverent and devout feelings. The idea is, that he was 'distinguished' among the works of creation, or so 'separated' from other things in his endowments as to work in the mind a sense of awe."[52]

Barnes continues, "He was made different from inanimate objects, and from the brute creation; he was 'so' made, in the entire structure of his frame, as to fill the mind with wonder. The more anyone contemplates his own bodily formation, and becomes acquainted with the anatomy of the human frame, and the more he understands of his mental organization, the more he will see the force and propriety of the language used by the Psalmist.i"[53]

---

[52] Barnes, Albert. *Notes on the Old Testament* (Grand Rapids, MI: Baker Book House Company, 1998), p. 294.

[53] Ibid, p. 295.

Flipping Over the Needlepoint

The human body is a bold indication that God has created and put together a weaving of colors, textures, mappings, and connectors within our body, soul, and spirit. This weaving was not done haphazardly, but with intentionality and purpose. Therefore, we must stop looking at the other side of the needlepoint and flip it over in order to get a glimpse of His divine beauty and grace in our lives.

The backside of the needlepoint may be in complete disarray. The crisscrossing of threads, the lack of form or shape, and the confusion of colors may be the description of where you are right now. We always seem to look at the backside, especially when the front side seems to be incomplete.

You should have the assurance that you are becoming, you are taking shape, and you are experiencing a makeover. When you're in the place of "this," it can mask your vision and becloud the process of God's masterful weaving in your life. As a result, you may become discouraged, confused, and hopeless. Without the consciousness of God's masterful orchestration, you may abort the process that produces the beauty, the wonder, and the majesty of God's glory being exercised in your life.

Who Gets the Credit?

The mystery of the tapestry of our lives is that we are not the ones doing the weaving. Truly acknowledging this mystery can either cause us much joy, or trepidation, depending on our perspective. If we have a true sense of our own humanity, we welcome the intervention and creativity of a Master Artist. When we tire of trying to accomplish and achieve greatness in our own strength, we can then wait with bated breath in joy and expectation for His fullness to bloom and blossom in our lives like a beautiful flower.

On the other hand, if we are stuck and grasping for the illusion of control of our lives, we may be dismayed at the humbling realization of how deeply we need Him. When we want to sit upon the thrones of our lives, we are often frustrated that the weavings and strings of tapestry are not our own work. We come to regret that we cannot claim ultimate credit for the glory and the greatness revealed, the "giftings" and the goodness in our lives. We have to yield control and give credit where it is due. We must reconcile ourselves with the fact that without God to initiate the work in our lives, we are hindered, hampered, and stagnant. We must release our desire to make things happen and our urges to weave our own tapestry.

For example, a woman may find herself in the position of having an unwanted pregnancy. Whether married or unmarried, Christian or atheist, women can find themselves having mixed feelings about the timing of a pregnancy. Being able to yield to the "timing and design" of the tapestry is challenging. What if you just accepted a new position and despite your happy marriage, a pregnancy is a surprise. How could God give you a baby to care for just when you have so many new duties on your job? Now is not the time you would have chosen for this. But, accepting the "timing and design" of God can bring great blessing. Letting God weave the tapestry at a time like this develops patience and character. Yes, there will be trials and tests. Having a baby is challenging, but God can see both sides of the tapestry and all the richness of His design.

We are the handiwork of a Master Artist. It is His workings, and not our own efforts that produce the beauty of the tapestry. Were we to have control of this process, the picture produced would be entirely different from God's original intent. Moreover, we would miss so many stitches, connections, and nuances that make a needlepoint artistically beautiful, or a life worth living. We would seek self-interest rather than divine understanding. Our work would be dimensionless and flat. Yet we as the creatures must reconcile ourselves with the handiwork of a sovereign Almighty Creator, and find in His purpose the beauty and grandeur of what we take for granted.

The Placement of the Needle

The beauty of needlepoint is to understand the placement of the needle. Why does the artisan place the needle there? What is the intention for each stitch? Within the seemingly random artistry, there is order. For every piece of needlework, there is a pattern that must be followed to produce the precision and the perfection of detail in the final picture. However, there is a paradox. From our limited perspective, we only see one side of the tapestry as the needle is placed. We only see the underside. But the underside is often displayed as a mass of confusion and even ugliness. Stitches cross randomly and without any semblance of order, form or beauty.

When we consider our lives in the context of this disorder and disarray, this is what often causes us much pain and distress. We view the underside of our lives and cannot grasp a glimpse of God's ultimate purpose in design. Yet we must not lose sight of the Lord's intention, or allow ourselves to be distracted by a season in our lives that we do not understand. We must be confident in the Master Artisan, Who sovereignly places the needle where He wills, selects colors and arrangement as He sees fit, and holds our lives securely in His control.

The Sovereign Artisan

The sovereignty of God is a central, fundamental concept that must be understood as we address His work in our lives. He is the Potter and we are the clay. He is the Vine and we are the branches. Without Him, we can do nothing. Sovereignty speaks of God's absolute rule. He needs to consult no one in His workings with His creation. Yet man in his delusion would like to think that he is God, "the captain of my soul," as declared in William Ernest Henley's poem, "Invictus":

Out of the night that covers me,
Black as the Pit from pole to pole,
I thank whatever gods may be
For my unconquerable soul.

In the fell clutch of circumstance
I have not winced nor cried aloud.
Under the bludgeonings of chance
My head is bloody, but unbowed.

Beyond this place of wrath and tears
Looms but the Horror of the shade,
And yet the menace of the years
Finds, and shall find, me unafraid.

It matters not how strait the gate,
How charged with punishments the scroll.
I am the master of my fate:
I am the captain of my soul.

Even when man understands that he is not God, he still grasps at the desire to be in charge, to exalt his will against God and think he has control over his own destiny. An extreme view of this humanistic philosophy can be seen in the popular Frank Sinatra song, "My Way," authored by Paul Anka, which alludes to man's desire to create his own tapestry, write his own rules, and chart his own course:

"To think I did all that;
And may I say - not in a shy way,
No, oh no not me,
I did it my way.

For what is a man, what has he got?
If not himself, then he has naught.
To say the things he truly feels;
And not the words of one who kneels.

The record shows I took the blows -
And did it my way!"

Yet man fails to realize that in his insistence and attempt to control and create his own tapestry, he does so imperfectly. He produces an imperfect and incomplete picture. He may produce his own design in his own willfulness, but it tampers with the view of eternity. It is then that he must live with the consequences and repercussions of his own designs.

At that point, man discovers the frustration and futility of having to live with his own imperfect tapestry, and its consequences. You and I must acknowledge that many times we have had to live with choices we have made that we knew were in direct defiance of the counsel of God. The repercussions of our choices; the reaping of our seeds sown we could only endure as we realized that we made our choices with our eyes wide open. Yet we have the audacity to complain to the Lord about the ugliness of our own self-made tapestries.

> The foolishness of man perverteth his way: and his heart fretteth against the LORD (Proverbs 19:3).

> And he gave them their request; but sent leanness into their soul (Psalm 106:15).

We must consider our ways and come to grips with a central truth — many times the Lord must graciously allow us to hit our brick walls. We often have to "bottom-out," before we see the error of our ways. Why would God allow us to try to weave our own tapestries and pursue our own course, knowing that it will end up in frustration and futility?

The best-known example of this is in substance abuse "recovery." People that are chronically addicted to mood-altering drugs and controlled substances often have to reach bottom before they can understand that their own choices are not healthy or beneficial. The drive can be so compelling that some drug addicts remain in "denial" for years.

When they are confronted with how destructive their behavior is to family, friends, and co-workers, they simply deny the severity of what is happening. Some addicts have to lose family, friends, their jobs and their dignity before they can even start to see the problem. Some addicts almost die before they come to their senses—which is another powerful reason to pray for them.

But for those who survive, by the time they realize that they cannot control the demon(s) of their addiction, many addicts have ruined their lives and sometimes even the lives of others. It is a tragic waste, but it is the only path to understanding.

But this suffering is not without a reason. It is so that man can discover in humility that ultimately, God, Who is majestic, awesome, and perfect in all His doings, is in charge. He makes no mistakes or errors. He never fails to accomplish or achieve His perfect ends. He holds us securely in His hand, and His grasp is not unsure, nor His grip weak. We must yield our lives to the tapestry of His work. We must agree with His doings (even when we do not understand them). As we yield our hearts to the sovereignty of His wisdom, expertise and excellence, we will see His glory fully revealed in our lives.

The Workmanship of Almighty God

For we are his workmanship, created in Christ Jesus unto good works, which God hath before ordained that we should walk in them (Ephesians 2:10).

As unique expressions of God's workmanship, we discover that we are the representations of His intricate craftsmanship. We are reflections of His limitless creativity; He makes us capable of introspection, perspective, and understanding.

Paul wrote to the church at Ephesus to draw a familiar comparison. Ephesus was known as the worship headquarters of the goddess Diana (also known as Artemis). Ephesus and its artisans had created a billion-dollar industry in fashioning shrines and images in homage to Diana for sale throughout the known world.

Yet the workmanship, craftsmanship, and artistry displayed by these seasoned artists could never compare with the masterful hand of Almighty God. Those artisans were creating lifeless idols that could not save or create anything. The Lord's witting, masterful Hand uniquely and masterfully fashions and designs our doings, goings, and all our ways.

The Completion of the Tapestry

When the tapestry is complete, we are able to see God's glorious design. We see the beauty, the intricacy, and the excellence of His mighty work. Our lives are continually unfolding with the richness of the colors of the tapestry and design. Are you ready for the fullness of the design to be revealed in its entirety? Do you trust the hand of the Master Designer? Allow Him to exercise the fullness of His lavished love upon you, so that the height of the expression of the beauty of His creativity can be seen in your life. Be patient in the midst of the unfolding of the tapestry, quiet yourself and know that God will get you to the other side of "this!"

God, the Master Designer, often begins a tapestry in the most unlikely places. The mesh can seem a bit tattered, the color pattern uninspired and the silken threads dull. But that is only one side of the tapestry. Take, for example, the Book of Ruth.

Her husband and in-laws were foreigners in Ruth's homeland of Moab. They were in exile, fleeing a famine. But, Naomi, and her family, must have been people who walked with God in a manner that deeply impressed Ruth. When tragedy struck, and the men in the family died, one after the other, Ruth had to weigh her options. She was a young widow, and a Moabitess. Would she be like her sister-in-law Oprah, who wept over her losses, but decided to return to her family and gods? Or would she cling to Naomi and her God?

It seems that so far in the story of Ruth, one tapestry was woven, an ordinary one — a tapestry of marriage, widowhood, and loss. But, then, the Master Designer changed things. He presented Ruth with a decision. She had free will and she willfully chose God. With that choice, the Master Designer changed the tapestry from one of ordinary tragedy to a tapestry of celestial beauty. He used Ruth to weave a truly remarkable story.

Ruth chose not to return to her people, the Moabites, who were a notorious race of idolaters. She stood with her mother-in-law in the road and pleaded with her. Many of us have heard the verses of Scripture Ruth spoke, in the context of a wedding, without knowing that a joyous bride did not speak these words to a groom; a destitute widow entreating her mother-in-law spoke these words:

"And Ruth said, Intreat me not to leave thee, or to return from following after thee: for whither thou goest, I will go; and where thou lodgest, I will lodge: thy people shall be my people, and thy God my God: Where thou diest, will I die, and there will I be buried; the Lord do so to me, and more also, if ought but death part thee from me" (Ruth 1:16-18, KJV).

Naomi, who was filled with bitterness and grief, nonetheless allowed Ruth to come with her. The two women returned to Naomi's native Judea. The women were without status, as widows, and they had no money or means. Yet God was willing to prepare a way for the women to not only survive, but to thrive. Upon their return to Judea, Ruth not only found a way of supporting herself and her mother-in-law, she found a kinsman-redeemer. How often do we find that we are in a position where we have lost everything we thought mattered: status, money, friends — a lifetime's work destroyed or lost — and there in the midst of despair is a Redeemer?

In ancient times, a widow could be "redeemed" by a family member of her husband's clan. The kinsman-redeemer would "inherit" the dead relative's property and wife. The obligation of the kinsman was to have children for the deceased man, and these children would carry on his name and eventually inherit this property. However, not every kinsman wanted this responsibility, particularly where the estate would cost him more than he could afford to maintain it. This was the case for Ruth. Although she had found favor with a kinsman-redeemer (who was eager to marry her), there was another kinsman who was in a closer degree of kinship. The kinsman with the closest degree of relation had the first right to redeem.

The tapestry becomes an interesting weave here. How would the conflict resolve? What was God working on? How would the sharp contrast between the law, which required Ruth to marry the nearest kinsman, and her love for the man who redeemed her, be resolved? Was her devotion to God part of a dramatic work of embroidery?

As the story unfolds, the first kinsman refused to redeem Ruth, because it would have "endangered his estate." This cleared the way for Boaz, who loved Ruth and was eager to be her redeemer. In this dramatic turn of events, her beloved, Boaz, redeems Ruth. But there is so much more to the story. It is not just a "happily ever after" ending. Ruth gives birth to a son, Obed, who is the father of Jesse, who is the father of King David — the great king of Israel. Moreover, the full greatness of Ruth's tapestry is not revealed until many millennia later when the Messiah, the Redeemer of the world, is born into the earthly line of King David.

And so it is only after many thousands of years, that we see the full impact of Ruth's decision on the road to follow the God of Naomi. In her lifetime, Ruth saw a pleasing version of the tapestry. She was redeemed and she had a family—a husband, a mother-in-law and children. Her status in the community was returned and she was a respected woman. Ruth was satisfied with the tapestry of her life. But the full, awesome, celestial beauty of the tapestry was not seen until the life, crucifixion, and resurrection of the Messiah. It is a tapestry we can all adore. Her story of loss and redemption is our story. When she lost everything, and was left standing in the road, forced to choose, she chose God. We share in her story, because no matter how difficult our circumstances, we can choose God, who will take us safely through to "the other side of this."

Flipping the Needlepoint

Create & Design
After reading Chapter 5, answer the following
questions:

Design: Fearfully and Wonderfully Made
1. Loss is being exiled from the persons or things that
you love. How many times have you become depressed
in the midst of your exile experience? Explain one of
your most recent experiences.

_____

_____

_____

_____

_____

_____

_____

_____

_____

_____

_____

_____

_____

_____

_____

_____

_____

_____

_____

_____

Who Gets the Credit?
2. Are you willing to admit that you may be stuck and grasping for the illusion of control of your life? In what areas do you see this? Be specific.

_____

_____

_____

_____

_____

_____

_____

_____

_____

3. In what ways have you desired to do things your own way?

_____

_____

_____

_____

_____

_____

_____

_____

_____

_____

_____

The Completion of the Tapestry
4. We understand that "this" is the purpose and plans that God is orchestrating in your life. The Lord's witting masterful hand is uniquely fashioning and designing our doings, goings and all our ways. Can you begin to see the unfolding of the completion of the tapestry? Are you beginning to trust the hand of the Master Designer? How is your trust evident?

_____

_____

_____

_____

_____

_____

_____

_____

_____

_____

5. What interesting weaves are you seeing in your "this" situations? Briefly describe the complicated circumstances that make things appear hopeless.

_____

_____

_____

_____

_____

_____

_____

Spiritual Maturity

6. Can God use you to weave a remarkable story as He did with Ruth? What plan will you put in place to allow God to do His part? How will things change? How will your speech change to accommodate your surrender?

_____

_____

_____

_____

_____

_____

_____

_____

_____

_____

_____

_____

_____

_____

_____

_____

_____

_____

_____

_____

_____

_____

_____

_____

_____

Personal Inventory

Ruth chose not to return to her people. What choices will you have to make in order to accommodate the purpose of God in your life? What will you have to leave behind?

_____

_____

_____

_____

_____

_____

_____

_____

_____

_____

_____

_____

_____

_____

_____

_____

_____

_____

_____

_____

_____

_____

_____

_____

_____

Dr. Jacqueline E. McCullough

Glorious Connections

From the foundation of the world, God has been bringing forth connections. These connections are the conduit and the means through which the glory of God is revealed. Everyone has heard the expression, "For no man is an island unto himself." We neither live without inter-dependence nor do we accomplish the will of God by ourselves so that we alone get the glory. Indeed, we work together, bringing each of our gifts and talents together, so that we may accomplish the will of the Lord together.

In our modern, contemporary society, we see the power of connection through the phenomenon that has become known as "networking." Many people consider themselves to be professional "networkers." Through networks, individuals link together through common interests, attributes, goals, and/or visions. Business professionals extol the power of the network to create business empires, but even everyday people find social networking websites like Facebook, Twitter, and LinkedIn as powerful tools for interacting.

Yet why do we need the network? What does its existence say about the human heart? Networks simply demonstrate the human need for connection. Yet in the midst of all of these networks, links, relationships, and associations, the ultimate connection that the human heart longs for is with God the Father Almighty. Only He can satisfy our heart's cry for intimate connection.

The Election of the Lord

The Lord continues to boggle our minds by the methods and means He uses to establish connection. He usually works in a manner diametrically opposite to our will, way, and nature. When we seek human connections such as friendships, acquaintances, and associates, we often gravitate to those people with the most charisma, those with whom we have an affinity, feel comfortable with, or share some similar interests. Yet God often uses the least likely people, places, and things to orchestrate our blessing. It is a theme echoed six times throughout Scripture, beginning with David in the Psalms:

> "The stone which the builders refused is become the head stone of the corner" (Psalm 118:22).

To those words uttered by the lips of our Messiah:

> "Jesus said unto them, Did ye never read in the scriptures, The stone which the builders rejected, the same is become the head of the corner: this is the Lord's doing, and it is marvelous in our eyes?" (Matthew 21:42).

And, again, in the Apostle Peter's sermon in Acts 4:11, which following the ascension of the risen Savior, ushered 3,000 souls into the Kingdom:

"This is the stone, which was set at naught of you builders, which is become the head of the corner."

And, the final culminating proclamation in 1 Peter 2:7:

"Unto you therefore which believe he is precious: but unto them, which be disobedient, the stone which the builders disallowed, the same is made the head of the corner."

While we often look to the people we believe are most likely to succeed for our deliverance, many times the Lord selects and elects those whom we overlook. Through those exact connections we believe are "going nowhere," because they lack the charisma and status we believe matters, God makes His most powerful moves. Let's take a look at God's divine connections in action.

A Divine Connection

"And Elijah the Tishbite, who was of the inhabitants of Gilead, said unto Ahab, As the LORD God of Israel liveth, before whom I stand, there shall not be dew nor rain these years, but according to my word. And the word of the LORD came unto him, saying, 'Get thee hence, and turn thee eastward, and hide thyself by the brook, Cherith, that is before Jordan. And it shall be, that thou shalt drink of the brook; and I have commanded the ravens to feed thee there.' So he went and did according unto the word of the LORD: for he went and dwelt by the brook, Cherith, that is before Jordan. And the ravens brought him bread and flesh in the morning, and bread and flesh in the evening; and he drank of the brook" (1 Kings 17:1-6, KJV).

Elijah of Tishbe is the central character of this scriptural passage. In the midst of the wickedness of the reign of King Ahab and his idolatrous wife, Jezebel, the will of God was pronounced by Elijah, the prophet ordained to announce judgment upon the nation of Israel and its king. The prophet Elijah foretold a drought, which would consume the land and bring judgment on the people. What was the result of this judgment? There would be neither rain, nor dew for three years, except by the word of Elijah.

According to *Nelson's Bible Dictionary*, "Lack of rain brought famine to besieged cities."[54] So the drought did not have isolated impact, but brought famine, disease, and despair to all the people. It reduced the people to terrible unspeakable poverty, starvation and desolation.

In issuing the prophetic decree, even Elijah was not exempt from its surrounding consequences. The drought would also overtake the land in which Elijah went to hide from the murderous threats of Ahab. Despite his obedience to God, issuing the Word from the Lord would jeopardize Elijah's life in more ways than one. Not only was Elijah subject to the ravages of the drought and famine, the King of Israel was furious at him and put a price on his head. Yet God knew what Elijah was facing, and because of the urgency and importance of the pronouncement, God gave Elijah a

---

[54] Easton, M.G. *Nelson Illustrated Bible Dictionary* (Nashville, TN: Thomas Nelson Publishers, 1995), p. 245.

promise that would sustain him in the midst of judgment. The Lord promised to give Elijah food and water while God's judgment rested on all the other people of Israel.

It would not be the first time that the Lord would spare His chosen people in the midst of judgment all around them. In the time of Moses, when Pharaoh's heart grew stubborn, the Israelites in Goshen were spared the plagues that overtook their Egyptian neighbors:

> "And I will sever in that day the land of Goshen, in which my people dwell, that no swarms of flies shall be there; to the end thou mayest know that I am the LORD in the midst of the earth" (Exodus 8:22, KJV).

> "Only in the land of Goshen, where the children of Israel were, was there no hail" (Exodus 9:26, KJV).

As the skies grew like brass, refusing to give rain, God gave Elijah connections. But again, the connections were the most unlikely. The first connection was with the ravens.

Ravens are the largest birds of their class, yet were considered unclean by the Jewish people (Leviticus 11:13-15). According to *Nelson's Bible Dictionary*,

> "Ravens are scavenger birds that will eat almost anything. Their harsh cry has probably contributed to their reputation as birds of ill omen. Since they have keen eyes and strong wings, this may explain why the first bird Noah

sent from the ark was a raven (Genesis 8:7). "These birds were also known for their practice of pecking out the eyes of a body — a quick way to determine whether their meal was actually dead" (Proverbs 30:17)![55]

Yet from their interaction with Noah in Genesis, we see that the keen eyes and strong wings of these black birds only served their rapacious, greedy, selfish nature. Indeed, it is from their name and nature itself that we get the word "ravenous"! As Noah learned when he sent the raven on assignment, the ravens did not earn a reputation for dependability as messengers, but rather as self-serving creatures. Noah experienced the ravens' unreliability in the midst of the flood:

> "And it came to pass at the end of forty days, that Noah opened the window of the ark which he had made: And he sent forth a raven, **which went forth to and fro, until the waters were dried up from off the earth** (emphasis added). Also he sent forth a dove from him, to see if the waters were abated from off the face of the ground; But the dove found no rest for the sole of her foot, and **she returned unto him into the ark,** (emphasis added) for the waters were on the face of the whole earth: then he put forth his hand, and took her, and pulled her in unto him into the ark" (Genesis 8:6-9, KJV).

---

[55] Ibid.

The raven, functioning true to its nature as a scavenger, did not return to Noah to report, because its primary instinct was to feed itself. Surely in the aftermath of a worldwide flood, the raven would find a wealth of dead carcasses and flesh to feed upon. So the self-serving raven released itself from its responsibility to Noah and did not return to the ark. Unlike the dove, which returned to Noah to bring a report, the raven just kept flying throughout the earth. That's why the raven would seem to be the last bird God would select to feed His prophet in the wilderness.

It is striking that the ravens would be the ones to provide Elijah with food, in this most unlikely connection. It is almost inconceivable that God would use a ceremonially unclean bird to feed His holy prophet, and a violently selfish, unclean bird at that! Yet He did. Through His command, the ravens functioned contrary to their naturally predatory, rapacious nature, and instead, brought provision to Elijah in the form of bread and flesh in the morning and evening. So not only did these birds bring food to the prophet, they brought it regularly and repeatedly on a divine schedule to assure the well-being of the man of God.

Nelson's Bible Dictionary notes, "Because God sent ravens to feed the prophet Elijah, ravens are also associated with God's protective care" (1 Kings 17:4, 6).[56] It is notable that although the Bible records the owl, the kite, and the vulture, the Lord is not as concerned with other birds, except for possibly the dove and the sparrow, as He is with the raven.

---

[56] Ibid.

How could He give this bird such attention in view of its deeply sinful, selfish nature? Yet despite the unsavory nature of their character and personality, Scripture tells us plainly that the raven does not escape God's notice, consideration, and care. The Lord provides confidently and lovingly for all of His creatures. And He doesn't only love ravens despite their imperfections, but God even takes special notice of the young ravens (Job 38:41)! What other creature is deeply selfish and sinful in his very nature and yet benefits from the love and mercy of God? It is completely inexplicable, but it is surely the tender love and loving-kindness of the Lord for His creation! Oh, the wonder of it all!

What then can we learn from the raven? In the raven, we can see the Lord's provisional love for all of His creatures, whether clean or unclean. The Lord Jesus used a similar example to illustrate God's care for the most unworthy in Luke 12:24:

> "Consider the ravens: for they neither sow nor reap; which neither have storehouse nor barn; and God feedeth them: how much more are ye better than the fowls?" (KJV)

So the Lord used a "dirty bird" to function contrary to its very nature to assure that His prophet was sustained. God, not only can, but also does, use degraded things to accomplish His purposes. What we can learn from this is that we must never limit the Lord in who He may use to fulfill His perfect will and plan in our lives.

Surely Elijah the prophet would have preferred the Lord to issue His deliverance and sustenance by another agent. But it was a strategic time in a life-or-death situation and the Lord used the hunting and scavenging skills of the ravens. The ravens were not only acting contrary to their nature, they were on assignment from God. Those particular ravens had been consecrated for their task, even while they were unclean. Elijah had faith that allowed him to trust that God was using an unclean thing to accomplish a godly purpose. Had Elijah refused the food that the ravens brought, Elijah surely would have starved to death.

Who are the "ravens" in your life that may cause you to turn up your nose? It just may be this seemingly "unclean connection" where you will see the glory of God revealed. But do you have the discernment and insight to perceive the ways of the Lord in your life? Is "this" the time in your life to seek the Lord for spiritual vision to discern and receive from His connections, like Elijah?

Let's look again at Elijah's situation. The drought was designed to teach the wicked a lesson; yet, Elijah, who was innocent, was still suffering. The Lord used unclean things, the ravens, to bring about salvation when the sky was like "bronze" and the earth was barren, cracked and dry.

Are you in a situation where you are following God and still contending with "this?" What "unclean thing" might be God's agent? Remember, whatever "this" is, like the drought, it was not meant to go on forever. It was to be a temporary arrangement that Elijah would have with the ravens:

"And it came to pass after a while, that the brook dried up, because there had been no rain in the land" (Genesis 8:7, KJV).

Humbled, Brought Low, and Tried By The Fire

"And the word of the LORD came unto him, saying, Arise, get thee to Zarephath, which belongeth to Zidon, and dwell there: behold, I have commanded a widow woman there to sustain thee. So he arose and went to Zarephath. And when he came to the gate of the city, behold, the widow woman was there gathering of sticks: and he called to her, and said, Fetch me, I pray thee, a little water in a vessel, that I may drink. And as she was going to fetch it, he called to her, and said, bring me, I pray thee, a morsel of bread in thine hand. And she said, As the LORD thy God liveth, I have not a cake, but an handful of meal in a barrel, and a little oil in a cruse: and, behold, I am gathering two sticks, that I may go in and dress it for me and my son, that we may eat it, and die. And Elijah said unto her, Fear not; go and do as thou hast said: but make me thereof a little cake first, and bring it unto me, and after make for thee and for thy son. For thus saith the LORD God of Israel, The barrel of meal shall not waste, neither shall the cruse of oil fail, until the day that the LORD sendeth rain upon the earth. And she went and did according to the saying of Elijah: and she, and he, and her house, did eat many days. And the barrel of meal wasted not, neither did the cruse of oil fail, according to the

word of the LORD, which he spake by Elijah"
(1Kings 16:8-16, KJV).

The second connection was with the widow of
Zarepath. In ancient times, a widow was considered to
have no status. A widow was a woman who had no one
to provide for her. In fact, a widow was a woman who
could barely support herself. How could a woman who
could barely support herself provide for someone else?

To complicate matters further, this widow had a
son to support. And, if that weren't enough, Elijah
encountered her when she was so destitute and
impoverished that she was preparing to die! But Elijah
had already seen the sustaining power of the Lord.
Elijah had been sustained by ravens in a cave — he
knew that God could help him — even using a nearly-
dead, completely despairing widow.

Elijah commanded the woman to make him some
bread, as if she had abundant flour and oil to spare. The
widow, who was at her wits' end, obeyed him and made
him a cake of bread. Elijah ate, trusting in God. The
widow knew that Elijah was the man of God. Not only
was the widow Elijah's godly opportunity — Elijah was
also her only way of survival. The widow trusted God
more than she believed in her own desperate
circumstances. She, like the ravens, overcame her very
nature and her inclination to despair, and chose instead
to obey an invisible, but all-powerful Word at God's
command.

This widow was, not only, without status or
means, she was the "widow of Zarepath." Zarepath

means a "fiery place,"[57] and in the midst of drought and famine, a scorching, barren place does not seem to be a sanctuary or an oasis. How can it be that God had sent Elijah to a scorching barren place during a drought to seek out the most humble, impoverished woman in the land to help save His beloved prophet!

We have to recognize what Elijah and the widow learned from their desperate circumstances: *God is the only Sustainer.* God, in His vast creative power, is constantly making connections that allow His great sustaining love to be seen clearly. Jesus, Who loved and sustained all of creation with His great Sacrifice, tells us:

> "I am the vine; you are the branches. If you remain in me and I in you, you will bear much fruit; apart from me you can do nothing. If you do not remain in me, you are like a branch that is thrown away and withers; such branches are picked up, thrown into the fire and burned. If you remain in me and my words remain in you, ask whatever you wish, and it will be done for you. This is to my Father's glory, that you bear much fruit, showing yourselves to be my disciples" (John 15:5-8).

If we remain in Him, He will sustain us in "this." We have to see beyond our circumstances to our divine connection. Our connection to God is sustaining in a way that allows us to persevere in overwhelmingly terrible places and circumstances.

---

[57] Pfeiffer, Charles F. *Wycliffe Bible Dictionary* (Peabody, MA: Hendrickson Publishers, 1989), p. 1834.

But we are not only sustained by our connection to Him, we actually bear fruit. We get to see God working through us in the fruits of our labor. The widow was not the only one in her household who was saved. Her son, the fruit of her womb, was also sustained through her connection with God!

The Body of Christ

How do we "remain in" Christ in a way that we can receive the blessings that Elijah and the widow experienced as a benefit? The only real way to do this is to become part of His body — the Body of Christ. Many of us already belong to a church, but how do we use this experience to build our faith in a way that we can "remain in" Jesus?

First, it is important to understand that the Church is about people and their godly connections. The early Church did not consist of elaborate facades and beautiful buildings. The Church, in AD 70, consisted of people. The people who attended these early churches were literally the "living temple of God."

The Apostle Paul, in his letter to the Corinthians, reminds the early Church, that "...we are the temple of the living God. As God has said: 'I will live with them and walk among them, and I will be their God, and they will be my people'" (1 Corinthians 6:16). Christ has made it possible for us to have this intimate connection with God. We can, actually, have God dwell in us so intimately that we can find Him even in places that we didn't expect to find Him.

God knows us intimately. He knows our nature in the same way He knows the ravens' nature. Yet He overlooks our shortcomings and sees how much we need Him. Jesus is not confused about who we are.

His ultimate goal is to live in us and transform us into a temple of the Holy Spirit. God doesn't want to dwell in stone and stained glass windows; He wants to reside in "living temples." When we come together as the Church, we are the "living temple of God."

When we become a "living temple," God has fellowship in us, and through the Church, we become a family. Many of us come from deeply dysfunctional families. We have so many unresolved issues that we have neither eagerness nor motivation to start building a family with total strangers. To make matters worse, the late 20th century Church has gained a reputation as a judgmental and unwelcoming place, which has been rocked by continual scandal in the 21st Century. How can we ever hope to grow into a family in a place like that?

Second, we must understand that the Church is the congregation of God under a living Master Who is constantly engineering godly connections. Each member of the Church is a "lively stone." In 1 Peter 2:4-6, we read,

> "Coming to Him as to a living stone, rejected indeed by men, but chosen by God and precious, you also, as living stones, are being built up a spiritual house, a holy priesthood, to offer up spiritual sacrifices acceptable to God through Jesus Christ."

The Church is built of living stones, which are connected by loving-kindness, self-discipline and acceptance. "Wherefore, laying aside all malice, all deceit, hypocrisy, envy, and all evil speaking" (1 Peter 2:1), as a "spiritual house," each member of the congregation of God is a "living stone," properly fitted together to form the Church. But the Church is more than a "fraternity" held together by good works. The Church is where we individually and collectively build our connection to God because He has already built-up a connection to us.

When Christ was making His triumphant entry into Jerusalem, the religious authorities tried to humiliate Him by telling Him to stop the people from praising Him. But Jesus told them: ". . . 'I tell you,' he replied, 'if they keep quiet, the stones will cry out' " (Luke 19:40).

When the world stops praising, the "living stones" must rise-up and give Him praise! When we praise God, we become more than our dysfunction, or our dysfunctional background. We have the power, not simply to overcome "this," but we are enabled to bear fruit. Bringing forth and bearing fruit is required; when you know that you are a "living stone," you have the obligation to give and sustain in the way that the widow of Zarephath did. In the family of our Church, we become the "ecclesia," the "called-out." Our hardships don't define us anymore. Paul assures us that:

> "...we will no longer be infants, tossed back and forth by the waves, and blown here and there by every wind of teaching and by the cunning and craftiness of people in their deceitful scheming. Instead, speaking the truth in love, we will grow to become, in every respect, the mature body of him who is the head, that is, Christ. From him the whole body, joined and held together by every

supporting ligament, grows and builds itself up in love, as each part does its work" (Ephesians 4:16).

We must be joyful and rejoice that we have found connection and that we have not been left to ourselves.

Thirdly, we have to understand the role of our conduct in building godly connections. The Apostle Paul sent a letter to a young pastor of the early Church named Timothy. Just as the modern-day Church is struggling, the early Church also struggled with "connection." Paul in his letter was instructing Timothy about Church conduct, telling him that it was critical that "thou mayest know how thou oughtest to behave thyself in the house of God, which is the church of the living God, the pillar and ground of the truth" (1 Tim. 3:15, KJV). In this passage, the word "behave" is translated from the Greek word "anastrepho" meaning "to turn back, return, to sojourn in a place," denoting how "one walks around in life."[58]

Similarly, in the Old Testament, the young warrior David, in his early years "behaved himself wisely in all his ways; and the LORD was with him" (1 Samuel 18:14, KJV; see also vv. 5 and 30).

This would indicate the type of behavior that is born of a maturing spirit; we would engage in this behavior even when no one is looking. This is not behavior that is imposed on us from the outside; this is the behavior we display as a sign of our maturing character. The Church is comprised of people who have

---

[58] Zodhiates, Spiros. *The Complete Word Study Dictionary New Testament* (Chattanooga, TN: AMG Publishers, 1993), Greek word: *anastrepho, STC# 390*, p. 164.

167

been developing "godly character," as described in Paul's Epistle to the Ephesians, Chapter 2,

> "As for you, you were dead in your transgressions and sins, in which you used to live when you followed the ways of this world and of the ruler of the kingdom of the air, the spirit who is now at work in those who are disobedient" (Ephesians 2:2).

Yet, because God has showed us grace:

> "But because of his great love for us, God, who is rich in mercy, made us alive with Christ even when we were dead in transgressions—it is by grace you have been saved. And, God raised us up with Christ and seated us with him in the heavenly realms in Christ Jesus" (Ephesians 2:5).

And what are the "heavenly realms," but the Church? God lifted us, took away our reproach and made us "living stones." For that reason, it is important for us, who are set apart in this way, to know how to behave ourselves. It is God's grace that saved us, and it is our conduct as "living stones" which supports the Church in spirit. Our individual connection to the Church and God's congregation should be evident in our conduct. Our conduct ("anastrepho") opens us to deeper relationship with God and releases, through us, power to bear fruit.

Yet there is an even deeper reason for proper conduct (the "anastrepho") in the Church because the Church is the only "truth-bringer." The community of the Church is the "pillar and ground of the truth." A "pillar" is a basic support and the "ground" is the foundation of a structure. One is support and the other is foundation. Only the Church can support and defend the truth. The truth, in turn, is a great protection for each of us individually, and collectively. Jesus said, "I am the way and the truth and the light" (John 14:6). Jesus is the Beacon that can lead us through whatever "this" is in our lives that separates us from genuine connection.

Divine Interconnection, Joint Supplying Joint

The Church's connection is different from the goals of worldly "networking." The divine purpose of a church-body connection is to supply, edify, instruct, exhort, and support each other to produce a healthy, vibrant church.

> "From whom the whole body fitly joined together and compacted by that which every joint supplies, according to the effectual working in the measure of every part, makes increase of the body to the edifying of itself in love" (Ephesians 4:16, KJV).

Such a Church in turn would be well-equipped to execute the will of God with vigor, vitality and commitment. The weak, and almost insipid, organization that we call "church" is in that condition because of a lack of "joint supply" from the individuals who make up the church organism. Without a collective supply from each individual person who is filled with the Spirit of Christ, the Church becomes anemic, weak and ineffective. This is not a new challenge for the Church; even in Old Testament times, the people of God were faced with their collective and individual difficulty in building both their faith and their place of worship. The Book of the Prophet Haggai is a short book of only two chapters in which Haggai is sent by God to encourage and direct the "remnant" of the people that has returned to Jerusalem from the Babylonian exile.

The four messages of Haggai are: (1) that He is calling the people to rebuild the temple; (2) that the people are to remain faithful to God's promise; (3) that they are to be holy to enjoy great provision; and (4) that they are to keep their hope set on the returning Messiah.

By his prophecy, Haggai is covering the present time and a future time. He is directing his message to leaders of the Israelites, Jeremiah, the spiritual leader and Zerubbabel, the civil leader put in place by the Babylonians as a figurehead. Finally, the prophecy is also directed to the remnant people.

What is a "remnant"? Well, anyone who has ever bought fabric knows that the small amount of fabric left on the spool after most of the fabric has been sold is called the remnant. It is what's left of the larger, original piece.[59] So, after the entire people of Israel were sent into exile, as their punishment for their idolatry, only a remnant returned; that remnant was seeking God. They could have stayed in Babylon like the others, for, although the Israelites were bondservants there, life wasn't so bad; they could own property, marry, and participate in the civic and political process of the Babylonians.

---

[59] Merriam-Webster Online Dictionary, Copyright © 2012 by Merriam-Webster, Incorporated. http://www.merriam-webster.com/dictionary/remnant

But they couldn't worship their God the way they could if they had their own temple in Jerusalem. Most of the exiles chose to stay in Babylon, but the remnant was special—they wanted to return to Jerusalem and to their God. The remnant people were the people described by the Psalmist who "hung their harps on the trees" (Psalm 137:2). They could not live without godly connection.

But this remnant people, to whom Haggai was sent, were a people who were eager to return to what they believed would be "the good life." Like us, in the modern-day Church, the remnant had a fantasy. They wanted to return to the splendor of the temple of Solomon and the rich feasts that accompanied their religious observances.

They wanted God to take them "on a concord jet to the never-never land of eternal happiness." But instead they returned to Jerusalem and were greeted with hardship after hardship. The joy that the remnant people felt when they returned was quickly turned to discouragement. "This" thing that they were facing was discouragement. Like that remnant, our expectations of what God will do for us are quickly disappointed when we are confronted by our realities.

The first to become discouraged were the old men, because they had seen the splendor of Solomon's Temple when they were young men. The new temple of Zerrubabel was meager and spare. The old men groaned and lamented. This discouragement then spread to the younger people because they understood that the temple was spare; worse yet, they also saw that the harvest was spare. They wanted to observe the ancestral celebration of feast of Tabernacles with an abundant feast; instead, they only had a minimal harvest because the land had only been cultivated for a short time since their return.

But most discouraging of all, it seemed the prophecy had failed. The prophecies of Isaiah or Ezekiel were remembered. Isaiah 10:11 states: "In that day the Root of Jesse will stand as a banner for the peoples; the nations will rally to him, and his place of rest will be glorious." Ezekiel 10:4 also declares: "Then the glory of the LORD rose from above the cherubim and moved to the threshold of the temple. The cloud filled the temple, and the court was full of the radiance of the glory of the LORD." But how could that be? In Solomon's day, there had been a temple that was one of the Seven Wonders of the World! And now here was only a modest façade with very little gold or silver.

The economy had shifted. There was now scarcity where there had once been abundance. The economy had not aligned with the prophecy. "This" was a source of great discouragement.

But what do remnant people do when "this" happens? God sent a Word to them, and He sends a Word to us through a prophet whose name means "Festive."[60] The four messages of Haggai are: (1) He is calling the people to rebuild the temple; (2) to remain faithful to God's promise; (3) to be holy to enjoy great provision; and (4) keep their hope set on the returning Messiah. His prophecy is covering the present time and a future time—the latter house and the former house.

---

[60] Pfeiffer, Charles F. *Wycliffe Bible Dictionary* (Peabody, MA: Hendrickson Publishers, 1989), p. 793.

The prophet had to prophecy to a gloomy people. God responded to them by encouraging them to be strong. "Yet now be strong, O Zerrubabel, and be strong, Joshua, for I am with you!" (Haggai 2:4). Either you believe this or go get drunk! Either you believe this or go get on anti-depressants and give up! You have to believe this now; in the midst of things getting worse, be strong! Tell your soul, "Be strong!" If God is with you, that means He is committed to making the connection and He is committed to making the connection work for you! As believers, our greatest strength is to have God on our side.

God is a covenant-keeping God Who not only saved the Hebrews out of the oppression of the Egyptians; He saved your ancestors. So here are the people returning from exile with only a few resources in search of a merciful God. The harvest was spare and it seemed that the prophecy was unfulfilled. Unlike David and Solomon, there was no one to dedicate a fortune to the rebuilding of the temple; God alone is with them. How could they come through a time like "this" with only God? Well, when God is with you, who can be against you? The people had to trust in God. They had to be encouraged. They had to recall the days when God was performing miracles. God saved their ancestors! In a time when everything tells us that failure is at hand, we have to turn to God's Word for our strength:

"Then I thought, 'To this I will appeal: the years of the right hand of the Most High." I will remember the deeds of the LORD; yes, I will remember your miracles of long ago. I will meditate on all your works and consider all your mighty deeds. Your ways, O God, are holy. What god is so great as our God? You are the God who performs miracles; you display your power among the peoples. With your mighty arm you redeemed your people, the descendants of Jacob and Joseph. Selah'" (Psalm 77:10-15).

Read the Scriptures! God saved the Hebrews from the cruel hand of Pharaoh, He delivered the Israelites from the Philistines, He destroyed the mighty Assyrian army when they besieged Jerusalem, and He fed a prophet and a widow through a long drought with only a jar of oil and small portion of flour. His hands are not slack, nor His arm shortened. Our God is able to deliver us. Listen to the testimonies of the people in your life, and in your family, who talk about the miraculous strength of the Lord.

The Glory of the Latter House

The glory of the "latter house," the temple God built in His people, was going to be greater than the most magnificent facade. God moves in progressive ways.

He starts in one manifestation because He is heading to His ultimate goal, a deep and intimate connection. The "latter house" is a house of hope and connection and not discouragement and disconnection. Our discouragement overtakes us when our expectations are disappointed; we are disappointed because of our limited understanding and vision. God had to increase our understanding and prepare His people. He had to put something greater in us because "greater is he that is in [us] than he that is in the world"

(1 John 4:4). God wants to put His glory in His people. It is better to learn the right lessons on the way up to His glory, so we can be ready. If the remnant had gotten a beautiful temple, they might never have learned to overcome disappointment or how to be patient — they would never have established their connection with God.

It is God's good pleasure to provide for us. It is the glory of the "latter house" to seek God and a close connection with Him. Once our relationship is established, our lives are changed. When we are in the latter house, our destiny can be accelerated. When we are God's Temple, He can heal us in an instant. He can revive us in a moment. He can take away the taste for alcohol, or an intense lust, or a deep discouragement in the twinkle of an eye. The glory of the latter house says you can have peace, change, healing, promotion, and miracles. The latter house is always greater than the former house. It is not the beauty of the shimmering gold, or the chandelier, it is the light on the inside.

It is progressive latter-house experience that brings us through "this," because something greater is waiting—a latter-house manifestation is about to happen to a remnant house with a connection to God. In Psalm 24:9, the Lord says: "Lift up your head, O ye gates; and be ye lifted up, ye everlasting doors; and the King of glory shall come in."

If God woke you up this morning, He is giving you another opportunity to overcome discouragement. Fight back! No one is forcing you to feel bad. Be encouraged — encourage yourself in the Lord!

Do what's right, in spite of your feelings. Your feelings may tell you to quit, or lose your temper, or become anxious, but the Word tells you to "be still and know that he is God" (Psalm 46:10). If you can handle your feelings, you will have more power than a president. "He that is slow to anger is better than the mighty; And he that ruleth his spirit, than he that taketh a city" (Proverbs 16:32).

We may sin and do wrong, and it is in our nature to fall short of God's glory. But in order to overcome, we have to choose to honor the sanctity of our connection to our God. If we don't control our emotions, our emotions control us. Put God first; put what is right as your focus, rather than your emotions. Discouragement and depression are a choice. The people in the world who don't know Jesus don't have choices. They have no means to overcome the leading of their emotions — lost in the world, they have to obey their emotions.

When we have Jesus, we have power to choose. God sent His Son so that our sins can be forgiven. We have to choose His love. Jesus brings us hope. We are, or could be, the remnant that is enduring the hardships of following God despite the temptation to be discouraged. To get to the other side of "this" we need a genuine encounter with God.

Let's look at what one person who had a genuine encounter with the Lord, and what she was able to accomplish; she imparted life to a city, and lifted the pallor of religious oppression. The "woman at the well" had a heart-wrenching, life-changing encounter with the Lord Jesus Christ. She was a remnant of her people who encountered God.

At the beginning of this narrative, we find Jesus in an unusual position. He is alone, unaccompanied by His disciples and He is in Samaria. Jewish holy men, rabbis, and priests did not usually go to Samaria. In fact, the Scripture tells us that Jews did not associate with Samaritans. But most surprisingly, we find Jesus talking to a person with no social status, who was considered far beneath Him. This woman was the equivalent to someone or something "unclean," like the raven, which is an unclean bird. He not only talks to her, He asks her to draw water for Him to drink. The Samaritan woman recognized her own lowly and despised status. Like many people in the Church today, she may even have been fearful of being judged or accused. She asked Jesus in John 4:9-12,

> "You are a Jew and I am a Samaritan woman. How can you ask me for a drink?" (For Jews do not associate with Samaritans.) Jesus answered her, "If you knew the gift of God and who it is that asks you for a drink, you would have asked him and he would have given you living water."
>
> "Sir," the woman said, "you have nothing to draw with and the well is deep. Where can you get this living water? Are you greater than our father Jacob, who gave us the well and drank from it himself, as did also his sons and his livestock?"

Jesus goes on to reassure her that He is not only properly addressing himself to her; He tells her that if she knew who He really was and why He was with her, she could *ask Him* for water! But this reassurance makes her even more skeptical. By inviting her into a relationship of connection, Jesus is suggesting that He has the power to change all the rules. He has the power to change everything. So she asks him, "Are you greater than our father Jacob?"

> Jesus answered, "Everyone who drinks this water will be thirsty again, but whoever drinks the water I give them will never thirst. Indeed, the water I give them will become in them a spring of water welling up to eternal life." The woman said to him, "Sir, give me this water so that I won't get thirsty and have to keep coming here to draw water" (John 4:13-15).

The Samaritan woman is eager for the connection with Christ. She knows that He is greater than Jacob. She doesn't want to be thirsty over and over again; in other words, she doesn't want to be trapped in the things of the flesh that only satisfy for a little while. She doesn't want something temporary, she wants a lasting connection; one that is "welling up to eternal life."

But Jesus challenges her because He knows that there are many things in her life that are temporary and unsatisfying, including her marriages:

> He told her, "Go, call your husband and come back."
>
> "I have no husband," she replied. Jesus said to her, "You are right when you say you have no husband. The fact is, you have had five husbands, and the man you now have is not your husband. What you have just said is quite true."
>
> "Sir," the woman said, "I can see that you are a prophet. Our ancestors worshiped on this mountain, but you Jews claim that the place

where we must worship is in Jerusalem" (John 4:16-19).

Jesus knows her sinful past, Jesus knows that she has failed at connection and relationship; she knew He was all-knowing, but she was discovering that He was also merciful and willing to connect with her. He knows that her connections have failed her. There is a Jewish *Midrash*, which refers to the five Books of Moses, called the Pentateuch, as the "husbands."[61]

Even the Law of Moses had failed to make a connection to this woman, because the Jews had no dealings with the Samaritans. She admits her failure. But He allows her to go beyond her failure, allowing her to ask how she could worship, knowing that the Mosaic Law had restricted and constrained her to a lowly status. Knowing that she can't worship God where the law would require her to, she asks Jesus "must we worship in Jerusalem?"

Here is where Jesus reveals to her the redemption she has been waiting for all her life. Here is where Jesus tells us who we are as the Church. Jesus tells the Samaritan woman who is struggling to understand the awesome possibility that she is in God's presence,

> "A time is coming and has now come when the true worshipers will worship the Father in the Spirit and in truth, for they are the kind of worshipers the Father seeks. God is spirit, and his worshipers must worship in the Spirit and in truth" (John 4:23-24).

---

[61] Baumgarten, J. *Jewish Literature*, 2008
http://www.jewishvirtuallibrary.org/jsource/judaica/ejud_0002_0013_0_12632.html

Let's take another look at Jesus' agenda. He not only came to see about a woman, but to change a religious system of worship — a social system of prejudice and restriction. He then goes on to challenge and correct the bias of the Samaritan people and to elevate the minds of His disciples from legalistic religious thinking into a genuine understanding of the Kingdom of God (John 4:27-42).

How was this accomplished? He would use the most unlikely woman of all from a small village, known only by her geographical location as "The Samaritan Woman." He connects with her, she connects with Him, she connects with her people, and the people in turn connect with Jesus. Then through this experience, Jesus connected with the disciples in a more profound and powerful way. They began to bear fruit. This incident changed John the writer of this account.

He began to bear fruit when he wrote this account, which still bears fruit and changes lives to this day, more than 2,000 years later. Spiritual connection changes the world and its systems forever.

A Review of Revelation

Let's look again at how Jesus brought the Samaritan woman to her place of personal revelation, and gave these steps for connection:

First, Jesus makes her aware of the importance of getting and staying connected. He gives her the opportunity to exceed her circumstances and develop a connection to Him without judging her. She was eager to stay connected. A few chapters later, the Gospel writer recounts the parable of the vine. The

Samaritan woman believed and because of her faith she immediately bore fruit. When the others questioned her, she was able to answer their questions, because she has a connection to Jesus, to the Vine (John 15). **Second, before she could even testify, she had to endure the pruning process.** Jesus confronted her about her sinful past and her failures. The Lord challenged her about the life she was living. She confessed that it was all true. She confessed; she didn't boast, she confessed. She knew her lifestyle limited and restricted her. Her life of sin kept her subject to a law whose requirements she could never meet. She let herself be pruned by repentance (See John 15).

Third, her repentance enabled her to bear fruit, giving life to others. Her testimony stunned her fellow Samaritans because they knew she had led a sinful life. John the Baptizer gave a formula for bearing instant "spiritual fruit" as he told the Pharisees who were coming to be baptized to "get away from me you brood of vipers! Bear fruit that is consistent with repentance" (Matthew 3:8). The transformation of the Samaritan woman as proof enough for her community that she had been in the presence of God. That day, she gave birth to hundreds, possibly thousands of "spiritual children."

Fourth, it is also likely that the Samaritan woman was accustomed to making petitions for help. She had very little status and lived at the mercy of those who were more powerful. She petitioned Jesus when He gave her the opportunity. Prayer is a critical part of how we build a connection to God. Philippians 4:6 tells us, "Do not be anxious about anything, but in every situation, by prayer and petition, with thanksgiving, present your requests to God."

Prayer gives us both peace and power. As we develop a prayerful relationship with God, we become aware of our ability to pray on behalf of others. Prophets and patriarchs prayed on many occasions in Scripture on behalf of the people. Abraham, Moses, Esther, Jeremiah, David, and many others prayed to God on behalf of the people. Jesus prayed for Peter. The Holy Spirit intercedes for us continually before God. One of the great gifts of connection we get from God is a strong, consistent prayer life.

Finally, the Samaritan woman was ready to meet God, because she was well acquainted with the stories of her heritage. It is highly unlikely that she could read, but she had heard the stories of Jacob and Joseph and she knew her "spiritual heritage" even though it was humble and degraded. How many of us can say we know our "spiritual heritage" as well as she did? We can obviously read, and yet how many of us have taken time to do Bible reading, studying, memorizing, and applying with full obedience the way the Samaritan woman tried to do? We need to know and understand the Word of God because it prepares us for connections with each other and with God.

Once we have had an encounter and a connection with God, how do we go about bearing fruit? Yes, our testimonies are very powerful; but there is more. Giving, sharing, and serving with our families and with the Body of Christ, locally and globally, puts us in position to build greater connection with God. Earlier in this book, we learned that kindness can not only improve our immediate surroundings, it is singularly capable of ushering us into eternity. There is great power in godly connection for the faithful believer.

When we are in Church, worshipping in spirit and in truth, we are in God's presence. In His presence, He can begin to dwell in us more fully. When we worship Him in spirit and in truth, we can see His miraculous connections at work transforming our circumstances and re-making us. And, it is through godly connections that we, as a "maturing generation," can get to the other side of "this"!

Glorious Connections

After reading Chapter 6, answer the following questions:

The Election of the Lord

1. Noah learned when he sent the raven on assignment, that the ravens did not earn a reputation for dependability as messengers, but rather as self-serving creatures. Can you identify some of the least likely persons that the Lord is using to orchestrate your blessing? In what way were these people unlikely?

_____

_____

_____

_____

_____

_____

_____

Spiritual Maturity: "Humbled, Brought Low and Tried by the Fire"

2. How is God's selection of unlikely persons humbling you?

_____

_____

_____

_____

_____

_____

3. In identifying those with whom the Lord is connecting you, how are you overlooking their shortcomings as Christ does for us?

_____
_____
_____
_____
_____
_____
_____
_____
_____
_____
_____

4. You are a "lively stone" in the Church of the living God; therefore, you have the life of Christ, His gifts, His Word and His life pulsating in your heart and mind. Discuss how you can give or continue to give back to the Body of Christ and become truly connected to the Church's purpose in the Earth.

_____
_____
_____
_____
_____
_____
_____
_____
_____

Personal Inventory

Do you feel as if you are alone and overwhelmed in your "this" situations? If so, you could be excluding the people to whom the Lord is divinely connecting you. What is your plan for change in this area? Be specific.

_____

_____

_____

_____

_____

_____

_____

_____

_____

_____

_____

_____

_____

_____

_____

_____

_____

_____

_____

SATISFACTION OF THE SOUL

by Jackie McCullough

When looking at the condition of our world, it is not difficult to notice that people are seriously deficient of a genuine display of love. Because of that, people are often compelled to try and find love by drastic means. Many people try to satisfy themselves with illicit sex, drugs, fame, fortune, and power to fill that void. Their search unfortunately leads them down a spiraling path to even greater feelings of emptiness, rendering the whole quest hopeless. Although it may sound supercilious, there is only One that holds the exclusive rights to bring satisfaction to your soul: Jesus Christ.

105 DAYS OF PRAYER

by Jackie McCullough

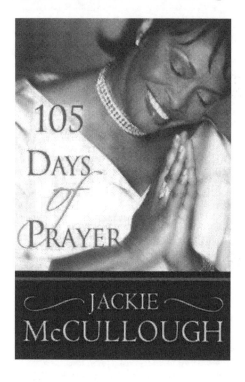

105 Days of Prayer offers guidelines on how to pray to God from a posture of true intimacy. A true prayer warrior has the honesty to seek Him from vantage of vulnerability. The open honest heart enables us to submit to God's will, and let His Kingdom come and His will be done.

DAILY MOMENTS WITH GOD

In Quietness and Confidence

by Jacqueline E. McCullough

As you journey into God's presence, take this volume with you. Author Jacqueline E. McCullough has compiled her very own treasury of poetry, punctuated phrases, and sermonettes to inspire you to trust, love and obey the Lord Jesus Christ. **Daily Moments with God** will direct your thoughts toward God, shed insight on the Scriptures and encourage you to embrace life from God's perspective.

To order your personal copy of **Daily Moments with God**, *please visit www.amazon.com.*

About the Rev. Dr. Jacqueline E. McCullough

"There is gold, and a multitude of rubies:
but the lips of knowledge are a precious jewel."

(Proverbs 20:15)

With an unwavering commitment to the Lord Jesus Christ, the integrity of His Word, and a love for God's people, the Reverend Doctor Jacqueline E. McCullough is a woman in pursuit of the Kingdom of God.

A second-generation preacher, Rev. Dr. McCullough is the senior pastor and founder of The International Gathering at Beth Rapha, "Where You Can Experience Healing to Heal by Loving Christ," in Pomona, NY. Her vision for evangelistic ministry is expressed in the international reach of Precious JEM Ministries, a non-profit religious organization, where she serves as President and CEO. Through this ministry, Dr. McCullough travels throughout the world ministering the Gospel of Jesus Christ and providing evangelistic tools such as books, tapes, DVD's, etc. to hungry souls around the globe. Dr. McCullough is also the Founder and President of the Beth Rapha Bible Institute, also in Pomona, New York.

Dr. McCullough was awarded her Doctor of Ministry degree from the Drew Theological Seminary, and currently holds a Master of Arts degree in Philosophy from New York University. She has also engaged in postgraduate study at the Jewish Theological Seminary. She is widely noted for excellence in ministry, including recognition from Ebony and Gospel Today magazines as one of the most influential African-American preachers in the nation.

A native of Kingston, Jamaica, Dr. McCullough also spearheads the WordAlive Medical Mission, which has provided free medical clinic services to over 30,000 people in parishes throughout the Island of Jamaica since 1997.

A prolific author, her *105 Days of Prayer*, a book of unconventional prayers from Destiny Image Publishers, was a best seller. Dr. McCullough's previous release from Destiny Image entitled, *Satisfaction of the Soul*, may be found in bookstores across the country and even in classrooms in Bible colleges and theological seminaries around the world. She is also the author of a daily devotional entitled *Daily Moments with God: in Quietness and Confidence* from PneumaLife Publishers.

For more information on Rev. Dr. McCullough, please visit her website at www.drjackiemccullough.org. You can also follow her on Facebook and Twitter.

The Official Rev. Dr. Jacqueline McCullough

DrJMcCullough

45363014R00107

Made in the USA
Middletown, DE
01 July 2017